We the People

New Socialism for a Modern World

A Brief Discussion About Freedom

by Martina Sprague

I0420671

Copyright 2015 Martina Sprague

Acknowledgements:

Front cover image: Martina Sprague

Back cover image rose: Peggy Greb (USDA-ARS), reproduced under Wikimedia Commons license. The red rose is a symbol of love; it is also a symbol of social democracy.

Back cover image horse logo (slightly adapted): CoralieM Photographie, reproduced under Wikimedia Commons license.

Other books of interest by Martina Sprague:

For God, Gold, and Glory: A History of Military Service and Man's Search for Power, Wealth, and Adventure

Leadership, It Ain't Rocket Science: A Critical Analysis of Moving with the Cheese and Other Motivational Leadership Bullshit

Sweden: An Illustrated History

Norse Warfare: Unconventional Battle Strategies of the Ancient Vikings

Swedish Volunteers in the Russo-Finnish Winter War, 1939-1940

TABLE OF CONTENTS

PREAMBLE

We the People of the United States, in Order to form a more perfect Union, establish Justice, insure domestic Tranquility, provide for the common defence, promote the general Welfare, and secure the Blessings of Liberty to ourselves and our Posterity . . .

—The Constitution of the United States

Society is a complex organism that cannot function effectively without a shared social structure, such as public schools offering quality education, public transportation, quality healthcare, social assistance to those in need, and a vision of the future that makes allowances for people of all socioeconomic backgrounds. Although political change takes time, the intended direction the country is moving should be clear. Neither extreme right nor extreme left viewpoints should be excluded in political debates; however, when all is said and done the ordinary citizen should have something of value to strive toward, and in the moment of decision his or her wishes should be heard. To this end, the masses must be active participants in the formation of the future and receive fair representation in all areas of concern.

Because of the dynamism of civilization, politics is a living entity with the aim of reaching a better future guided by the wishes of the people. Democratic socialism is a branch of politics that is built on certain core values, the first of which is the development of a society that openly embraces equality and social justice through powerful action. In this brief analysis, we will define our understanding of democratic socialism and also discuss what it means to the ordinary citizen when we say that we want to be free of government interference. To reach our objectives, we will build on the ideology of former prime minister of Sweden, Olof Palme, who many view as the epitome of social justice, and question the extent to which his ideas have merit and can be implemented in modern American society.

Who was Olof Palme? Olof Palme was the speaker of the Social Democratic Workers' Party in Sweden from 1969 to 1986. He was the prime minister of Sweden on two separate occasions, from 1969 to 1976 and from 1982 to 1986. Social justice, gainful employment for all, gender equality, and disarmament for peace were the major issues that dominated his political career. What made him such a remarkable political figure, however, was not his position in favor of a democratic socialist country, but his simultaneous anti-communist and anti-imperialist views. By challenging these dominant ideologies, he managed to upset both the far left and the far right on the political spectrum.

In the early 1970s, Palme worked primarily with developing labor laws related to the hiring and firing of employees, collective bargaining agreements, employee rights to a hazard free work environment, and employee rights to maternity, education, and sick leave. He argued that gainful employment was necessary for women, if they were to achieve social equality with men. Women could only reach financial and social independence, he argued, if they no longer had to choose between staying at home with the children and working outside the home.

Although Palme worked incessantly toward the elimination of a class structured society by decreasing the wage gap between rich and poor, providing care for the sick and elderly, and fully accepting and integrating immigrants and minority populations, he simultaneously believed that the individual should have the right to determine his or her own road to happiness. A decent home and access to education, a decent job and the right to a pollutant free environment, lay at the base of his definition of individual freedom and were rights that every human being should enjoy.

Outspoken, committed, energetic, and accomplished, Palme often stirred controversy on the international circuit and became an important political figure worldwide. He was against war in any form and argued that the United Nation's statute pertaining to war in self-defense was often used to justify military action where none was needed. He accepted large numbers of political refugees, worked tirelessly to liberate Third World countries from oppression, and presented a constant challenge to the Western world, not the least the United States, on issues that obstructed international action to a peaceful resolution to conflict.

In light of the fiery political debates since President Barack Obama took executive office in the United States, particularly with respect to social issues such as universal healthcare, affordable education, and the rights of workers to organize, this brief analysis sheds light on a subject that many Americans do not understand and even fear, or at least have failed to examine in depth. *We the People: New Socialism for a Modern World* is of interest to scholars of political ideologies and popular social movements; people with left-leaning views; and lay persons wishing to learn about the forces that stir politics in America today.

Olof Palme took a gigantic step when he left his upper middle class background and dedicated his life to the promotion of democratic socialism and human rights. Even those who disagreed with him often developed a love-hate relationship with him. On the international scene, his strife against war and oppression of the poor and underprivileged earned him the moniker, Citizen of the World. To what extent were his ideals sound and how might they impact twenty-first century politics in America, as we move toward yet another presidential election and the hope for a more inclusive and modern society?

WHO WAS OLOF PALME?

"I am a democratic socialist," said Olof Palme in a party leadership debate in 1982. He became a democratic socialist when he traveled in India and witnessed the extreme poverty of the masses alongside the extreme wealth of a few. He became a democratic socialist when he saw, in a sense, an even more degrading poverty in the United States; when, as a young man, he came eye-to-eye with the persecution of large numbers of people living under the oppressive regimes of the Eastern Bloc communist states; and when he visited the Nazi concentration camps in post-World War II Germany and was introduced to lists of union members and advocates of social democracy who had received death sentences for their beliefs. He became a democratic socialist when he realized that a focus on social justice was a factor directly responsible for lifting Sweden from poverty and unemployment during the economic crisis of the 1930s. "But more important," he said, "is that I gain strength in my conviction when I see the wars in the world, when I see mass unemployment, the corruption in my own country, the growing inequality between rich and poor, and when I witness how egoism rules our nation and social justice becomes a more fragile concept with each passing day."[1]

Palme embraced democratic socialism fully first after going through a careful process grounded in long study and deep thought. There was no single moment when a light came on, so to speak. "It was good to adopt a belief in social democracy gradually, and base this belief on continuity and realistic reasoning," he later confessed. "Naturally, this process did not exclude a strong emotional engagement."[2]

Although born into an upper middle class home, the young Olof Palme confirmed through words and actions that his heart belonged to the working class. His beliefs were formed by personal experience coupled with the time in which he lived. Born in 1927 into a conservative family, he became interested in politics at a young age and worked with Sveriges Förenade Studentkårer (United Students of Sweden) on international issues. His work involved considerable travels throughout Asia and many of the war-torn European nations.

Although his total embrace of democratic socialism came after careful and considerable study, he received his first insights into social structures, poverty, loneliness, and human suffering when traveling in the United States and Mexico upon graduating from Kenyon College, Ohio in 1948, which he had attended on a scholarship. After his time at Kenyon College, he hitchhiked across the American continent to encounter American society firsthand, and said later that this experience taught him more about life and society than any book ever could. A particular eye-opener came when he entered the ghettos in the southern states, and sat on bar stools face-to-face with ordinary people discussing their problems.[3] He believed there were two ways to come to terms with important matters: theoretical discussion and social reality. He viewed the latter as the more realistic of the two, and considered his travels in the world decisive for shaping his future views.[4] It was also at Kenyon College that he undertook the challenge of powerful public speaking, of arguing his cause convincingly. He returned to Sweden a new man, politically aware and with a growing sense of self-confidence.[5]

Palme's main motivation in his political endeavors was a belief in the need for an educated and united labor force with the strength to face the problems of the future. He got his first big break when he was hired at the age of twenty-six as secretary to Prime Minister Tage Erlander in 1953. He became the speaker of the Social Democratic Workers' Party in 1969 (see also Sveriges Socialdemokratiska Arbetarparti; Socialdemokraterna [the Social Democrats]; or simply *Sossarna* [popular Swedish slang]) and shortly thereafter prime minister of Sweden, and thus laid the foundation for the Swedish welfare state. His political career spanned thirty-three years, until his untimely death by a gun-wielding assailant on a street in Stockholm in 1986.

In the late 1950s, nine months before the 1960 election and soon after Palme took his first steps as a member of parliament, he began an ideological campaign to raise money for pensions for all, laborers as well as professionals. The development of schools, hospitals, and roads required funding, but he was fully aware that suggesting a tax hike would be political suicide. He started by asking the people to choose between consuming more goods or having access to better education and greater security in old age. Since any social program requires a monetary sacrifice, the wishes of the people must be heard. The result when the votes were tallied gave the Social Democratic Workers' Party a "second wind," which allowed it to recover from the weaknesses it had suffered during most of the 1950s. The votes revealed that the "consumer" hoped for a future that was grounded in the strength of the family, a secure place to live, education, employment, and a social safety net that covered illness, unemployment, and old age.[6]

Palme's political career was thus launched, and his early ambitions revolved around seeking an answer to problems of social injustices within Sweden. He believed that how other countries viewed Sweden was determined primarily by how Sweden treated the weakest members of society. In a speech to demonstrators against the Soviet Union's march into Czechoslovakia in 1968, quoting Ernst Wigforss, a prominent politician of the Social Democratic Workers' Party and a person who Palme admired, Palme stated that the difference between democratic socialism and communism was foremost the value one placed on the rights of the citizens. In a democratic socialist state, the individual has the right to protection against oppression by the power hungry elite; he or she has the right to free speech including the right to criticize the government; and he or she has the right to form with others a political majority that can implement the changes needed to drive society forward.[7]

Palme recognized that education was the key that would unlock the door to a healthier society and bridge the economic gap between rich and poor. The problems of the future must be attacked from a standpoint of equality, he argued, and bridging the economic gap would prevent a new class society from gaining a foothold in Sweden. Equality and social justice were not merely words, but were tangible conditions directly attached to the future of politics.[8] Sweden's long history of poverty and political oppression of the common man no doubt influenced his views. In fact, the Social Democratic Workers' Party, founded in 1889 when Sweden was an antiquated state run by free farmers, nobility, and priests, taught the common man how to organize for collective strength and demand social justice and a guarantee that every person could live his life with dignity.

Palme learned the importance of honesty and perseverance from his mentor and then prime minister of Sweden Tage Erlander, with whom he worked for sixteen years. He realized that to maintain integrity, a politician must view thoughts, words, and actions as a single entity.[9] His moral conscience required that privileged groups already in existence should be abolished and a watchful eye kept on the rising power of the elite.

Bridging the economic gap and preventing a new class society from forming thus proved important for the long-term growth of a state in which every citizen could prosper. The problem was that when the economic gap between rich and poor was large, those who fell behind, in order to secure their own well-being, would start regarding those better off with suspicion and animosity. And those better off would be on constant guard against the poorer people of society, whom they viewed as leeches obsessed with obtaining handouts from the pocketbooks of the hardworking elite. This would indeed be a difficult world to live in, Palme acknowledged, even for those ahead in the game. He expressed his views with ease, both orally and in writing. His fearlessness allowed him to become an anchor for society's underprivileged and weak.[10]

Palme further believed that social justice must precede freedom to live one's life to its full potential. The type of freedom upon which a democratic society is built means freedom for everybody and not only for a select few. It requires that every person's basic needs are satisfied, including the need for a decent place to live, and the need for access to quality healthcare and education. Children should get a satisfactory start in life regardless of the socioeconomic background of their parents, he argued, and universities should be planned so that they can accommodate large numbers of students hailing from all conditions and circumstances, rich as well as poor. He acknowledged that competition is important to move society forward; however, every citizen should be granted the same starting place by attending the same basic school. Society then has an obligation to compensate the less fortunate by offering assistance, such as tutoring by specialty teachers, to children from difficult socioeconomic backgrounds. The underlying principle of Palme's strife was the open admittance that all people have equal value. It is not enough that all are equal before the law, he argued. All must also have equal opportunity to choose how to live their lives. But to succeed with such a premise, we must first ask why equality is missing.

Palme found that the conditions on the labor market is the first barrier to reaching a more just world. Gainful employment for all is necessary, because unemployment leads to higher crime rates, greater drug use, and more suicides, which in turn lead to less functional families. The right to work, to have a job is also closely related to human dignity and self-esteem. Particularly the young, when unemployed for a long time, lose all hope in the future. If new jobs are not created before old jobs are phased out, the class division of society is exacerbated until only two groups of people remain: those with a higher education who are ready to compete on the labor market, and the rest who are unneeded. This bigger "nightmare," as Palme called it, would create an "us" versus "them" mentality, and prove counterproductive to any hope of a better and fairer world where all can prosper.

An important hallmark of Palme's political career was his strife to elevate minority populations and those normally regarded as society's outcast, before offering tax breaks and other benefits to the elite. A wage earner analysis conducted in the 1960s revealed that as much as one-third of the population had exceptionally low income, despite the fact that most of these people worked demanding jobs that required a full forty-hour or more work week. (The no-more-than-forty-hour-work-week was instituted in Sweden by law in 1973.)[11] If income was determined at least in part by the amount of work performed, there should be no excuse for this group to reside at the bottom of the socioeconomic ladder. Furthermore, a successful democratic socialist state, he argued, can consist only of "us"; it has to be inclusive of all citizens if it is to be a base for solidarity and protection against poverty. The citizens of such a state should not only have a say in how the state is governed, but also a responsibility to protect the interests of one another.

As a result of Palme's efforts, the primary duty of Sweden's Social Democratic Workers' Party in the 1960s was to increase the people's active participation in issues that required the implementation of new ideas. Since power rests with the movement of ideas and not with the privileged elite, ideas provide the foundation of the democratic state. It is through ideas that politics becomes everybody's business, because when ideas are embraced, the commoners are empowered to make decisions that affect their lives. Before implementing changes to existing norms, citizens must be asked whether those changes are in agreement with already established social values. To enjoy a strong democratic state, we must also understand the true needs of the people. "If we shall succeed in our duty, we need will and knowledge, and it is knowledge that provides a stable platform and gives firmness to will," Palme said in a speech to Sweden's Social Democratic Youth Party in 1955.[12] Participation in politics and social processes further ensures that no citizen is left at the mercy of a few government officials. This is important, Palme argued, because when a few "experts" apply a single formula based on stated "facts," which they force the people to accept, the inevitable outcome must be power struggles, resentment of authority, and new divisions of society into "us" versus "them."

But he also recognized that action requires resources. He who believes that everything (education, healthcare, childcare) in Sweden is "free" misses the point, because "free" is not, and was never meant to be, sustainable. The resources needed to create a society in which all can prosper must come through taxation aimed at all citizens, but particularly at those who have the greatest resources and make the most money. The dream of a better future can only be reached through the people's increased cooperation and willingness to entertain the idea of a fair division of the national budget. A prerequisite for advancement toward better schools, healthcare, apartments, roads, and other infrastructure is that people are ready to sacrifice some of their monetary resources for the common good. When the masses are willing to get politically involved and start identifying their needs, a stronger society and greater security will seem less farfetched. It is not only achieving the end result that proves important, but the fact that people should have conscious knowledge of the values for which they strive. Bridging the economic gap between citizens further creates a sense of camaraderie and cooperation, which, in turn, results in greater ability to drive society forward. The problems of the poor must therefore be regarded as more important than the tax concerns of the already financially secure.

Palme was a skillful strategist. He understood how to use compromise to his advantage. A living democracy with national independence, he believed, is synonymous neither with communism nor capitalism. He developed a dislike of communism early in life. However, while he found it necessary to take a stand against the communist powers of labor organizations, he simultaneously understood that the paranoia against communists that existed in the United States also served a negative purpose by fostering feelings of suspicion against any slightly left-leaning political views, including Swedish democratic socialism, which, at the time, he had not yet fully embraced.[13] Early in his career, many people in Sweden called Palme arrogant, *Besserwisser*, and renegade or traitor to his social class. His opponents often perceived him as overly aggressive.[14]

Olof Palme's political life can thus be summarized as follows: In the 1960s he worked on formulating Sweden's welfare ideology; in the 1970s he spearheaded the social reforms that placed Sweden at the forefront of equality among Western nations; and in the beginning of the 1980s, in the midst of the Cold War, he promoted an end to military proliferation in the name of collective security.[15] He kept these ideas alive throughout his career and allowed the Social Democratic Workers' Party to prosper. But the pendulum's swing between Utopia and the apocalypse has always been short, and, as Palme said, every belief in a predestined future is dangerous.[16] To retain vitality, a democratic nation must constantly press the frontier forward, and the first responsibility of a political leader is a desire to listen to the voices of the masses. Furthermore, the value of a society is a direct measurement of the value we place on our people, along with the recognition that everybody travels essentially the same road from birth to death.

With the foregoing in mind, we will now dig deeper into the social issues that affect us on a daily basis, and look at why freedom is a "prison sentence" (figuratively speaking) to some, while others consider it a "god-given right."

WHAT IS SOCIALISM?

The social democratic ideology is this: to improve the existence of the people on a daily basis. The only way to accomplish this is by building a society based on social equality, social safety, and solidarity. This new world for which we strive should have roots in the wishes of the individual. But it must be managed; it should not be a fantasy world drifting freely without direction or anchor.[17]

—Olof Palme

Although the word socialism, or social democracy in modern speech, commonly has negative connotations, talking about ideologies is useful for bringing about discussions that help us define a path that leads toward our goal. Without a clear definition and the will to achieve the objective, little will get done. That we must define what we want before we can accomplish anything of value, is part of what Olof Palme meant when he said that politics is a living entity and the goal is always to move forward, to progress, to make things better, and never to be satisfied with the status quo. But improving our existence also requires the embrace of an honest and often brutal discussion of which ideas tend to drive society forward and which tend to halt progress. It is thus not enough to say that one is pro-socialism, if one does not also have a clearly stated vision of what this means and how to achieve the ends. Naturally, the same applies to those who are anti-socialism or pro- or anti- any other political ideology. The clear definition of the objective gives power to the vision and power to change society.

Let us start by using Olof Palme's Sweden as a model for our analysis and consider a word that is loaded with undefined meaning: freedom. Palme acknowledged that it is somewhat odd to view socialism as a restriction on individual freedom. When speaking of freedom, is it not obvious that we speak of freedom for all and not freedom merely for a select few, he questioned. By definition, equality is at the base of individual freedom, and when equality is missing, individual freedom is necessarily hampered.[18] Palme argued that to achieve equality, it is essential to assist those who are less privileged to reach a higher standard of living, and that this must be done before assisting those who are more privileged to rise even higher, for example, by cutting their taxes or increasing their pensions.[19]

In the mid-1950s, Sweden started on the road toward the welfare state it is today, where the main idea was to lift people from poverty and give everybody basic economic security. But building schools, hospitals, and apartments that lasted well into the future required the collective support of the people. Mandatory savings over a set period of years was suggested. But to function as intended, the process of saving and building capital must be democratic. The people must approach the idea with vigor to prevent the economic gaps between rich and poor from widening.

Although Palme was ahead of his time, Sweden as a whole began to catch up with his way of thinking during the economic upswing in the 1960s.[20] The time had come to take advantage of employment opportunities and ending a class structured society. Reaching the objective required constant work and the contribution of new and innovative ideas. Palme defined socialism as freedom from outside oppression, and freedom of the individual to develop his or her talents in accordance with his or her desires. To this end, technical developments would help rather than hinder in the achievement of the objectives by modernizing society, because modernity plus equality equals freedom.[21] Palme did not understand those who blamed technology for the loss of the so-called "idyllic past" that had never really existed, anyway. Simultaneously, he did not view technology as a solution to all of society's problems, but viewed it as a tool that challenged society to take responsibility for making improvements with respect to equality and solidarity.[22]

The basic principle of democratic socialism, then, was to modernize society through the power of the state, while striving toward equal opportunities for individuals to reach their dreams.[23] If the people were dissatisfied in the 1960s, it was because they believed that the modernization of society did not go fast enough. They were not dissatisfied with democratic socialism per se, and were well aware that they needed larger apartments, better public transportation, and greater access to education for all.[24]

Welfare, freedom for the individual to choose his or her own path, and social security, were some of the concepts Palme campaigned on early in his career. In the first seven years in his role as prime minister of Sweden, from 1969-1976, he would realize many of his goals. Sweden became one of the foremost proponents in the world of equality and social justice by significantly decreasing the economic gaps between rich and poor, and by helping women find gainful employment outside the home by increasing the access to childcare and other social services. The level of education rose, and workers had more say in issues that directly affected them. Sweden took a great leap forward also in foreign policy questions, foremost by taking an active part in issues regarding the Third World, and in promoting democracy in the dictatorships that still existed in Western Europe.[25]

Before we proceed, it is prudent to remember that to conservative movements, the term capitalism commonly conveys that ownership of the means of production is in the hands of the capitalists or private companies. Socialism, by contrast, commonly conveys that ownership of the means of production is in the hands of the state. But to Palme, these sorts of definitions lacked value. A reason why the Social Democratic Workers' Party managed to remain in power in Sweden for so long, was because it managed to convince the voters that equality and social justice could be reached also without giving up a belief in market driven economy and private ownership of business.[26] In Palme's view, capitalism was a type of citizenship that embraced only certain formal rights, while democratic socialism was meant to reach deeper and give each citizen, regardless of his or her background, access to the same rights.[27] The terms capitalism and socialism therefore do not have the same meaning to everyone, and the socialism of one country or particular era is not the same as that of another. How we interpret democratic socialism is largely based on the history of our country, and how political movements have shaped the cultural preferences of the people. Democratic socialism is thus more an idea structured loosely around a set of principles, than it is a particular political movement or party.

In a broad sense, however, as the name implies, we can say that democratic socialism embraces values that have to do with social issues (as in labor unions, healthcare, childcare, equality and social justice, environmental issues, etc.) in a democratic way by the people, for the people (as in universal suffrage, freedom of speech, and freedom of the press). In order to successfully implement such social programs, we need a strong economy that will pay for it. It is therefore misleading to suggest that "everything in a social democratic country is free" (as in free healthcare, free schooling), and equally misleading to suggest that a social democratic country is opposed to the free market. Without the free market, competition, and the motivation to work, we can obviously not have a strong economy. People must obviously have the purchasing power to stimulate the economy. The trick lies in the balancing act; in good management of the free market along with the embrace of social programs.

At its core, then, democratic socialism is a struggle for the people, but a struggle through transparency, without secrecy or concealment. The people must always be the final authority on change. As previously noted, politics is a living entity and the idea is always to move forward. But the prerequisite for advancement is that people feel secure and that there are practical solutions to the problems of income and gender inequality, unemployment, and worker rights. Many factors interfere with personal development; for example, poverty, illness, and social needs. The pioneers of democratic socialism have stated that "[f]or a people to feel free and secure, the reasons that lead to poverty must be defeated . . . All people should have ownership of employment, a place to live, and ability to provide for themselves and family."[28]

THE JUSTIFICATION OF THE STATE

Olof Palme's socialism was neither about government controlled business, nor lack of individual initiative. Contrary to traditional socialism in the form of collectivism, the type of socialism Palme strove for was about the individual's relation to the state, where the state and the individual formed a sort of alliance.[29] The fact that the state held the resources for social insurance, health and sick care, pensions, and education would result in greater freedom for the individual; it would not restrict freedom, as was believed in countries that tended toward capitalistic ideals.

In a speech in 1956, Palme's mentor and then prime minister Tage Erlander demonstrated how individual freedom and personal development necessarily require a government effort and support by the masses. For example, if we are to own cars, then those cars must have roads to drive on; if we are to get a decent education, then we must invest in research and schools. This also means that we must contribute with resources to build these roads and educational institutions.[30] The freedom of the individual is therefore directly related to the efforts made by the state. Furthermore, to hold citizenship in a society means that we must interact with and influence the lives of other citizens, just as they must interact with us. Our lives are therefore formed by the lives and actions of those around us.[31] Once this is understood, we can easier see how democratic socialism does not restrict individual freedom, but contributes to greater freedom for the individual. The individual can reach greater autonomy over his or her life when he no longer must depend on the good will of family, friends, churches, or employers for his welfare, but on a less personal and almost anonymous state; universal, in fact, and ruled by law.[32]

A key value of Palme's beliefs was thus the rights of the individual, the ability of each person to form his or her own future. This is perhaps the issue that is the least understood when we talk about socialism in the United States. As Palme explained in a speech on employment and welfare at Harvard University in 1984:

> The purpose of society is not to realize any singular idea, unrelated to the conditions of human life. It is not to be built for the yonder, nor as a goal in itself to manifest the greatness of the nation or the state, nor in the interests of any particular group or class. It is not to be built according to any rigidly determined blueprint for the perfect society of the future.[33]

In other words, since every person's ambitions and dreams differ, a clearly defined ideological state, or a Utopia if you will, cannot exist. Although we can certainly dream about a perfect future, we cannot attain it, because, as individuals, we are too diverse in our dreams and wishes. This realization makes it impossible to impose a sort of "straitjacket" on society that is inflexible and follows a specific ideal. It also bears to remember that the government is created for the people; not the other way around. A truly democratic society, by its very definition, prevents the government from imposing any type of Utopia on the population.[34]

Palme further communicated that everyone cannot be grouped under the same umbrella. Although he believed in equality, individual freedom, and generally in the modern Western world's political ideas, he disliked both laissez-faire-liberalism and totalitarian systems of government. As a pragmatist, he avoided taking a hard idealistic stand. He understood that political problems must be solved through compromise, which often meant being prepared to give a little in order to gain a little.[35] He further understood that although Utopia differs for all and depends on what we want from life, everyone should be granted the capacity and resources to live a rewarding life where our dreams can be realized. Building a nation worth living in is never a finished project. Reaching better living conditions requires constant work, and whichever method we apply today cannot necessarily be applied tomorrow with equal success.

Although many ideologies strive for the type of Utopia where rules are created for the achievement of the common good, and although Swedish socialism has roots in Marxism, the idea that Swedish democratic socialism has anything to do with communism today is archaic. Nobody in a modern democratic socialist nation admires such individuals as Joseph Stalin, for example.

Once we understand the balance that must be struck between ideology and pragmatism, we will naturally see why freedom for some is also a limitation of freedom for others. To illustrate further, in a lecture on social justice and individual freedom at Stanford University in 1977, Palme explained the pride the Swedish people took in *allemansrätten* (everyman's right), a freedom granted by the Constitution of Sweden, that gives every citizen access to all areas of nature, regardless of private ownership. Every citizen has the right to roam freely in the mountains, the forests, the lakes, and has the right to pick wild berries and mushrooms that grow in nature. Although this law does not grant anyone the right to destroy property or disturb nature, it does give every citizen certain rights that potentially place limits on somebody else's "freedom" to buy a forest, or an island, or a lake, for example, or any other piece of land and restrict access by the rest of the population.[36]

The choice that must be made is this: Do we want freedom for all to enjoy nature, or do we want freedom only for the tiny elite who can afford to buy themselves a part of nature and restrict everybody else's access? Ultimately, the choice is a balancing act and may depend on which social class one belongs to. As a whole, however, the Swedish people treasure this right to universal access, and families typically spend every free minute out in nature, whether in a forest, on an island, or on a beach. Likewise, a fundamental building block of a democratic nation is the equal right to vote and the idea that no one can buy additional votes or increase their voting power, no matter how splendid their financial situation. Since the millionaire elite is normally small in number compared to the middle and lower classes, in any transparent democracy, a vote on an issue similar to *allemansrätten* would likely fall in favor of the masses, who cannot afford to buy themselves a private island or forest.

Although socialism is about the value we place on the individual, the bigger question is, how is this achieved? Palme used to say that the function of any ideology or political objective, in accordance with Polish philosopher Leszek Kolakowski's ideas, is not to reach it, but to strive toward reaching it.[37] When money alone rules our lives, the economic and social gaps between rich and poor will necessarily increase.[38] To Palme, the idea was to create a society where nobody would fall through a crack in the social safety net. Since he had grown up on Östermalm, one of the most affluent areas near the Swedish capital of Stockholm, his life took an interesting turn when he embraced socialism. His family enjoyed certain privileges normally not afforded the commoners and also had a rather conservative worldview. That Palme turned away from his family's political inclination after he had seen the misery in the world, demonstrates that he was an independent thinker. But he also inherited many admirable traits from his immediate family; for example, a desire to view the world scientifically and from a modern perspective, an interest in and ability to speak foreign languages, and a strong interest in literature, drama, and rhetoric. Last but not least, he inherited the conviction that to reach our goals in life, our willpower must be mobilized in a clear direction.[39]

While all of this sounds good in theory, socialism cannot be limited to a word and many barriers must be crossed. How do we, for instance, justify the high taxation of the welfare state in relation to freedom and individual liberties? When moving toward the political left, one of the more common questions of concern surrounds the tax code, and a mere mention of raising taxes can easily lead to political suicide. But how do the high taxes the socialist Swedes pay compare to the taxes we pay in our capitalist United States? For instance, when daycare centers in Sweden became widely available along with education for adults, the cost was of course higher taxes, which rose to 10 and even 15 percent higher than taxes typically paid in other Western countries.[40] Simultaneously, when we talk about lower taxes in the United States, we often do not consider the fact that we have to pay separately for childcare, education, and healthcare, and a lot of other benefits that are included in the taxes paid in Sweden. Overall, when these benefits are accounted for, Swedes and other Scandinavians rarely pay higher taxes than Americans.

Palme argued that the relatively high taxation that the welfare state and social reforms demanded should not be viewed as a check on individual liberties. It was never meant to be a government takeover, as some might have feared. Rather, it was the opposite: a way to increase individual liberties. Without the opportunities the social welfare system brought to the individual, such as opportunity for education, decent housing, and good employment, people could naturally not exercise their liberties and fulfill their dreams. But in order to prevent divisive attitudes, the opportunities provided by the state must be provided to everybody equally, and not only to the poorer people of society.[41] This may be one of his greater insights.

A universal welfare state, in which everybody participates through taxation and draws the same benefits, will eliminate the notion that the rich are paying for the poor, while simultaneously being forced to find private solutions to their own problems. In order to give everybody, and not just the needy, the full advantage of the welfare state (and thus gain the support of the masses, including the support of the wealthy), it must operate without a profit motive. Equally important is that when everybody participates in building a society that is just, individual participation in government and decision-making processes will also increase and prevent the possibility of a so-called government takeover of individual liberties.[42]

After three decades in politics and only two years before his untimely death, rather than talking about what had been achieved, Palme considered what was still left to be done. A study of the differences in income and capital between people revealed the enormous workload that still lay ahead. Viewing politics as a living entity with a strife for improvement helps explain why it is more important where we are headed than from where we have come.[43] Although raised in nobility, Palme dedicated his life to the promotion of democratic socialism and lifting the poor and powerless from poverty and misery. His upper class socioeconomic background was important only to the right-leaning parties, to those who liked to talk about and criticize his policies. But it was not important to the democratic socialists he represented.[44]

What made Palme so interesting was thus his relentless pursuit of his vision and his stubborn refusal to give up. He constantly stirred controversy, which was also what made him so effective. Controversy moves people to action and, as Palme said, politics cannot function unless there is action and constant movement in the direction toward our goals. As we well know, political issues that stir emotions generally resonate with the people. But Palme also demonstrated why these emotions were based in logic, which made them difficult to ignore after the initial fury of the debates had settled. He argued that the state/government was not, as those to the right on the political spectrum claimed, an entity that slowed down progress and inhibited opportunity to live life as one chose, but rather an entity by the people, for the people and necessary for building better infrastructures, caring for the citizens in their old age, and providing standards in education for all, rich as well as poor. The job of the government was not to inhibit individual growth and initiative, but to promote it by making available the resources the people needed. It was through the access to higher education that the social equality gap could more easily be closed.

And how is this important on a grander scale? How has it moved through time? Palme noted that in Europe, in the early days of the industrial revolution, labor issues and how one fared economically were largely a result of individual management of money and the economy. How one fared was largely related to how disciplined one was with managing one's personal finances and how well one planned for the future. The government neither had the responsibility nor the means to guard the people's personal welfare. If one were rich, it was because one had worked hard and managed one's resources well; if one were poor, it was the opposite, because one had been lazy or spent money too lavishly on unimportant things.

With the foregoing in mind, it was not so much his ideals that made Palme such a spectacular politician, but his ability to articulate them in a way the people could understand and that gave them hope of a better future; a society that was more just with greater equality between rich and poor, male and female. When the concept of democratic socialism was clearly articulated, attitudes changed, and it was generally acknowledged that how one fared had a whole lot less to do with how well one managed one's personal finances, and a whole lot more to do with how society affected the individual. If all people were to prosper or at least be socially secure, society as a whole must change and not just the individual person.

The acknowledgment of certain facts makes this argument easier to understand. When we are children, we all depend on others for our basic needs. Likewise, most of us will at some point get sick and be unable to work, at least temporarily. Even those who manage to remain in good health will eventually grow old and be unable to continue working.[45] It therefore makes sense to plan for the hardships that will inevitably befall most of us at one time or another. When the government assumes the role of planner for these misfortunes, the individual will no longer be dependent on charities or benevolent handouts, and will thus realize greater freedom.

In the 1960s, the younger generations in Sweden shifted their views to where they no longer considered a person's value related to whether or not he owned a car, a house, or a television.[46] The human being had an innate value that was unrelated to his or her financial situation or worldly goods. This way of thinking was one of many reasons why the people began to embrace democratic socialism and equality of opportunity for all. It was generally acknowledged that the state should hold the resources for individual self-actualization. When people had achieved basic security in the form of healthcare, pension, a place to live, etc., they should have the opportunity to seek an education, embrace culture and art, and become productive and valued citizens. The mere idea that the state had the capacity to help people become more self-sufficient and free had strong support in Swedish society.[47] Palme believed that how we build society is always related to the conditions of human life. We should not build in order to honor the building itself, but in order to improve the human condition. "Society and its institutions are to serve people here and now," he said, "so that they shall be able to realize their life project, live their lives. Then they will threaten no one's future. Then people will go on building on the life experiences of earlier generations."[48]

When social welfare was debated in Sweden in the late 1950s, however, a paradox as an effect of optimism was noted: Achieving freedom, the possibility to plan for the future, buy a house and a car, and get good education for one's children, also made people more dependent on the government's help when sickness and unemployment struck. The challenge was to use democratic socialist policies to guarantee a preserved status of living also in individual times of despair. But to function, unemployment benefits, for instance, must be tied to an individual's prior earnings, so that he or she could maintain the standard of living he had achieved prior to the time that calamity struck. Social equality therefore did not mean the exact same compensation or benefit for everybody, but rather the same opportunity to preserve one's standard of living.[49]

As we have seen, freedom is an abstract concept that we tend to understand through gut feeling. But if asked to define it in concrete terms, the definitions are as varied as the individuals. As a young man in the United States, Palme came to understand how much economic growth and material acquisitions meant with respect to social relations within society. Freedom and progress came about as a result of individual opportunities to break with the daily grind and improve one's lot in life. The focus should therefore be on future opportunities as opposed to past losses. When the state has the power that the individual lacks; that is, the power to make the journey less inconvenient and more secure, people will no longer view an expanding government with disdain.[50]

When Palme's early mentor and former prime minister Tage Erlander passed away in 1985, Palme held a speech that summarized Erlander's idea of democratic socialism. In a single sentence, he explained that society (the state) should be strong so that the people do not have to be weak.[51]

WHY IS GENDER EQUALITY ESSENTIAL
TO A FUNCTIONING STATE?

Olof Palme started to focus on gender equality in the 1960s and found the gender gap significant in all areas of society, including politics, business, research, and technical fields. His work on this subject would place Sweden, more than any country in the world, at the forefront of gender equality. The reason why the gender gap was prevalent, he reasoned, had nothing to do with the biological differences between men and women per se, but with the fact that the biological differences were used to justify the division of duties. But if the principle of equal value was to be regarded as important, it was unacceptable that women, only because they were women, should have lower paying jobs and fewer rights than men. Rectifying the problem required more than a written law requiring equality between genders, however. It required a change in how the male gender viewed his responsibilities. When men felt that women were responsible primarily for the children and the home, women could not focus fully on working outside the home and gaining financial parity with men.

Sweden was treading on new and unknown ground. Since most countries of the world suffered greatly from issues of inequality, both in general and especially when it came to women, Sweden had no opportunity to study and learn from others. Palme reasoned that since people are part of the society in which they live, large gaps not only with respect to income and social equality, but also with respect to gender equality, will hamper not only the poor and the female half of the population, but everybody's ability to get along and feel welcome and needed. When this happens, solidarity can no longer develop and grow.[52] When social and gender equality do not exist between rich and poor, male and female, society will soon disintegrate and be no society at all. It will create an "us" versus "them" attitude, where egoism and greed are at the forefront of all our decisions and actions. Since many factors other than the economy influence social equality, living as equal citizens requires more than declaring everybody equal before the law.[53] Equality on any scale is thus not a question of me or you, my kids or your kids, but rather a question of us and our kids together.

To Palme, equality on any level was not simply a political choice between capitalism and socialism. He realized in the early 1970s that in order to move forward on social issues, he needed to energize the voters by organizing the women, the most often overlooked part of humanity. Sweden was full of dissatisfied women who wanted to take work outside the home but had no one to care for their children. Society had developed to the degree that housewives were no longer looked kindly upon. Simultaneously, a mother with small children at home could not assume work outside the home, because somebody had to care for the children. It was a catch-22.[54]

What had made Sweden one of the least housewife friendly countries in the Western world was tax reform that hit the parliament in 1971. Until then, a married couple's income had been taxed jointly, which meant that if the wife did not work, the family got bigger tax breaks, since the husband could make use of the wife's standard deduction in his tax declaration. But if she took employment outside the home, she would get taxed at a higher rate, since she had an income jointly with her husband. With the new tax reform, husband and wife paid their taxes separately and independently of each other.

Tax reform and the modern way of thinking about family values also allowed men and women to live together and have children without getting married, and without getting penalized with higher taxes for not being married.[55]

At a party congress in 1972, Palme's courage became evident, not so much because of what he said as because of the fact that he dared to bring to light and debate a question that most politicians shied away from. He explained that nobody could nor wanted to forbid anyone from being a housewife, and that both individuals and couples had every right to determine on their own how best to care for their family. The importance of the matter was that keeping women confined to the home did not resonate with the principle of gender equality, because as long as the woman remained a housewife, she would continue to be subjugated on the labor market with lower wages, less security, and a poorer education; all because of the one motivating factor which held that she could go back to the home whenever she chose and be cared for financially by her husband. Although Palme's initiative led away from the values we traditionally place on the family and focused instead on women's role in the labor market, he managed to join gender and political questions in a way that mobilized the working classes to action.[56]

The question of gender equality was not new; however, any political idea takes time to develop. As early as 1961, a Swedish journalist named Eva Moberg stressed that the opponents of women's liberation viewed women's rights to individual freedom only in relation to children's rights. A woman who wanted to reach self-actualization was viewed as antisocial, unnatural, masculine, and even inhumane. Rather than viewing the responsibility for the children as solely the mother's, the solution involved splitting the responsibility in three ways: between the mother, the father, and society. Contrary to popular belief by the opponents of gender equality, the family would not lose its value, but would remain one of the most important institutions of mankind. Our views must thus be changed to reflect the type of gender equality where both partners work, the woman is financially independent of the man, and the family receives support from the state with the children.[57]

Although Palme had no intent of deciding how couples should split their work duties and time, he meant that women should not consistently have to stand back when it came to jobs, wages, security, and education. He also meant that when it was necessary for one parent to stay at home with a child that was sick or required more assistance than others, society should provide the missing link by giving him or her the opportunity to take advantage of an important time to be with the child, without risking punishment in the form of job loss, demotion, or harassment when returning to the labor market later.[58]

This all sounds good in theory. But to avoid creating a failed world inadvertently, the question of why social and gender equality are missing in the first place must be investigated and answered truthfully. To avoid attaching value to outdated notions, such as the idea that women's role is in the home, a clear vision of the path that leads to the objectives is needed.

As in many Western countries at the time, the typical Swedish family in the 1950s consisted of a husband who focused fully on his career, and a wife who had to balance her own career with responsibilities to home and family. As Sweden moved into the modern era, although it was evident that women should have equal opportunities to higher education and access to traditionally male dominated occupations, it was simultaneously evident that women were still the primary caregivers to home and children.[59] Palme reasoned that in order to break this pattern, men must be required to carry half of that burden. If not, the state would have to step in and provide childcare in order to make full-time employment for women possible. In order for the individual to prosper, laws must thus be implemented that dealt with issues of childcare and elderly care, and enough people must be employed in professions that focused on meeting the needs of the very young and very old who required this care the most. Norms must be changed so that caring for fellow citizens would not be viewed as an unnecessary bureaucratic burden.

There was another problem, however, that must be confronted to break old habits and outdated notions. While both boys and girls were encouraged to study and get a good education so that they could get good jobs, for boys it had never been a matter of choice between work and family. For boys it was obvious, as they grew up, that they should take a job outside the home. For girls, on the other hand, the focus had always been on finding a decent man with a decent job, and then, just in case something went wrong, an education, too, which she could fall back on if needed, for example, if the man's job did not work out as well as hoped.[60] This kind of thinking naturally created problems, because if women had to carry the main burden of home and family, there was not enough time left for them to focus also on education and a promising career, even if by law they had equal access to both an education and an occupation. While men had only their careers to focus on, the burden of both home and career was too heavy for women to carry alone. If women were to leave the home in bigger numbers and go to the universities for a higher education that would lead to superior employment, a change in attitude of all members of society was needed.

But if women were happy caring for home and family and working perhaps part-time hours to make ends meet, why should a politician like Olof Palme get involved in issues that were private family matters?

Palme was a visionary leader who looked toward the future. When women have a good education that lead to a good job, he reasoned, discriminating against them at work or assigning them duties of lower pay and lesser status will become much more difficult. When women contribute more to the economy by earning a good chunk of the money, they will no longer depend on men for their existence and will thus earn political power. The reason why men are more prominent in politics and hold positions of decision-making power, is because women have traditionally provided men with these opportunities by staying at home. If women are to participate equally in building and contributing to society, they must also have the same opportunities and the same network of support that men are afforded, which means that men's role must change along with women's role.[61] Equality for women is thus not solely a female question.[62]

Palme further argued that as more women joined the labor force and moved toward financial parity, it would also have a positive effect on men. When men were forced to assume a bigger share of the duties that were formerly considered women's work, such as home and childcare, society as a whole would change, forcing greater support by the state to families where both parents worked. More and better daycare centers would be needed, and/or shorter workdays so that working parents had more time to spend with their children.[63] In order to get women to join the workforce, they must be given the knowledge and confidence that their children would be cared for through government sponsored childcare, and that they would not lose their jobs should they get pregnant with another child.[64]

The motive to change society was driven by ethics. Since mothers traditionally carried the heaviest burden in the family, school lunches for children and daycare centers were instituted, allowing women to join the workforce in greater numbers. Education and work outside the home gradually allowed women to reach financial independence, which further led to the abolishment of man's role as primary bread winner and supporter of the family.

The extent to which a country truly embraces gender equality can thus be measured against the extent to which it is willing to turn politics to action, and the extent to which it uses political will to make the necessary sacrifices that lead to a change in outdated notions. In theory, it is not so difficult. When determining which policies to embrace and which to reject, we must only look in the direction we desire to move; we must only ask which issues are discussed in politics and where the votes are won. But in practice, solving the problem of gender equality does not only involve taking active steps to move women into the workforce and into positions of power. The male population must also be educated, so that they understand that equality for women leads to a better life also for men and for their children.

Palme's interest in gender equality is understood as a part of general equality. The idea is that no person should be subjugated to another, whether in working life or within the family, nor internationally with respect to colonial interests. Socialism is about freedom from dependence on a class society. The privileged minority has always had freedom to choose their path in life. The purpose of democratic socialism is to broaden this freedom to include every citizen, male and female.[65]

It might be interesting to note that despite Olof Palme roots in nobility, Hanna Palme (born von Born), married to Sven Palme, the paternal grandfather of Olof Palme, was engaged in political questions, such as women's suffrage as well as military conscription for women, a full two generations prior to the Sweden that Olof Palme would come to lead. In addition to being engaged in the bigger political questions, she took an interest in making the traditional female chores easier by suggesting practical alternatives, for example, to the long skirts and dresses that were popular in the nineteenth century, and by introducing a dishwasher that would relieve women of the long and boring procedure of washing dishes by hand.[66]

AFFIRMATIVE ACTION FOR GENDER EQUALITY

A reason why there was and still is so much resistance to women gaining equality with men, is because it is viewed as a zero-sum game, where more power for women is thought to mean less power for men.[67] But the only way to end discrimination against a particular group of people, whether women or blacks, is for these groups to have the same earning potential as the group that is traditionally viewed as superior. Political power and thus equality rests with the ability to make money, to be able to support oneself and one's family, to be financially independent of handouts from church groups and other charities, or from family and friends, and also to be financially free from dependence on a spouse. In order to achieve this objective in a highly unequal society, the state must take an active part in promoting and providing the means for underprivileged groups to break free of their social inheritance and enter a new and more fair world.

The debate about equal pay for equal work encountered quite a few stumbling blocks in Sweden, as it did and still does in the United States. A common notion is that women earn only 77 percent (or so) of what men earn. But to gain clarity and insight into the situation, two separate issues must be investigated. First, we must ask whether women work in the exact same occupations as men, and if they do in fact work the exact same number of hours. If we do not know the answers to these question, the opponents of gender equality will argue that women earn less than men because they choose to work in occupations that do not require the same knowledge or education, or because they choose to work fewer hours in the same job, and not because their hourly pay in the same job is less per se.

If, in fact, it is determined that women earn less than men because they work fewer hours than men, we must then ask why. We will likely find that the reason why is because women are frequently in charge of the home and family, and therefore cannot delegate as many hours as men to higher education that leads to a good job outside the home. Simultaneously, we must recognize that the only way for women or any minority group to reach parity with men (particularly white men) on any level is by gaining the same political power. Political power, or the power to influence decisions and improve one's situation, comes only by working outside the home and earning financial independence.

We thus resort to affirmative action in granting women better job opportunities. But even then, women can only take full advantage of it if all domestic chores are shared equally by men. Since children literally are the key to the future, this could present a difficult situation for both men and women who desire to work outside the home and also have children. It is interesting to note that while the United States has long-term energy and defense policies in place, and argue that these are necessary for the uncertainties the future may bring, there is no long-term policy for the welfare of the children, who literally are the future.[68] Palme recognized that an alternative way to break the archaic pattern of requiring women to stay at home, was to ensure that adequate and affordable childcare facilities and school lunches were available for all. Both parents would then be free to seek full-time employment outside the home, or go back to school and further their education for the prospect of getting a better job with a higher salary.

Palme spoke about these issues in 1977. At the writing of this book, a decade and a half into the twenty-first century, fathers in Sweden are required to use at least a substantial part of the paid parental leave granted to couples when a child is born. This allows fathers to truly assume the role of being fathers. The reasoning is that when the father has time to change diapers and feed and play and read with his child, both father and child will benefit and thus the whole family will prosper. When mothers join the workforce in greater numbers and fathers accept greater responsibility for their children, not just in economic terms but also when it comes to changing diapers and reading bedtime stories, society as a whole will benefit and become friendlier toward children. Palme argued that how we treat our children today affects how our country succeeds tomorrow. Fathers must do their equal share alongside of mothers, but society as a whole must also take shared responsibility by providing good daycare centers and schools. We should thus not think of children as my children and your children; they are society's children since, as a group, they provide our link to the future.[69]

Equally important is that when men are required to take their share of the combined paid parental leave and spend time with their infants and toddlers, employers can no longer claim reluctance to hire women because of the likelihood that women will be gone for long periods of time on maternity leave. As of 2015 in Sweden, "parents are entitled to 480 days of paid parental leave [390 of those days are paid at 80 percent of normal pay], and now 60 of those days are reserved for the father."[70] But, according to a new government proposal, beginning in 2016, men will be entitled to a third month of paid paternity leave.[71]

Then as now, those opposed to Palme's ideals of gender equality claimed that they were damaging to the traditional values of the family. Another common criticism of the Swedish welfare state is a lack of moral values through the breakup of the family by making women work outside the home. For example, the conservative American sociologist David Popenoe held the view in 1988 that Sweden, more than any country in the world, lacked all institutional ties that held the family together. The young were no longer dependent on their parents, and man and wife had autonomy before the law, and the elderly were cared for by the state. Palme did not view this as a problem, but said that through these societal improvements, people had become independent of economic interests they could not control.[72]

Affirmative action thus involves more than granting minority populations, such as women or blacks, priority when going to school or seeking occupations. Affirmative action means implementing initiatives aimed at taking firm and clear action to eradicate social problems of inequality as a whole. In Sweden, affirmative action also involved reaching equality in the government. Palme started to actively push forward in the question about gender equality in business and government in the early 1970s. Sweden at that time did not differ much from other European countries with respect to their views of women and women's place. Women were clear minorities in leadership positions both in business and government. The social democratic congress in 1972 had approximately 50 women out of (then) 350 delegates total; in other words, approximately 1 in 7 were female, which compares similarly to the United States government today more than forty years later, where approximately 19 and 20 percent of congress and the senate respectively is female.[73] Since then Sweden has come a long way. Today, Sweden has one of the most gender equal parliaments in the world, where very nearly half of the seats are held by women. This would never have happened had it not been for a concerted effort toward the achievement of this objective.

Our gut feeling tells us that gender equality is ethically correct in a modern world. But why, really, is it so important in government? The reason why is because no political party can function democratically if it is not equally represented by all members of society, men as well as women, rich as well as poor. At the very least there must be strife toward achieving equality, because an unequal party will necessarily represent an unequal population.

A graphic example of affirmative action "in action" is when the Swedish *Toys R Us* franchise adopted a gender neutral Christmas catalogue in 2012 (following a reprimand from the Swedish advertising watchdog agency a few years earlier), which included pictures of girls wielding toy guns and boys cuddling dolls.[74] By not picturing toys in gender roles, the hope was to destroy old traditional views of women's roles in the home. Kids can of course choose which toys they prefer, but society as a whole should not take a stand on which toys are appropriate for boys or girls solely based on their gender. A toy should not be viewed as a boy toy or a girl toy, but as a child toy regardless of gender. This example may at first seem irrelevant to democratic socialism, but is a clear continuation of the policies started in modern Sweden after World War II and built upon by Olof Palme.

Another example of affirmative action for gender equality is when Palme relieved the king of Sweden of his last power in a rewrite of the Act of Succession that went into effect in 1980. Rather than having the first-born boy succeed the king upon the king's death, it was decided that succession should be gender neutral and go to the first-born, regardless of whether it was a boy or a girl. At the time, Prince Carl-Philip, the second born, had already been titled heir apparent, or Crown Prince, but, due to the new affirmative action law, he had to relinquish the title to his older sister Victoria.

Taking affirmative action, then, means knowing exactly what one is striving for and staking out a specific path intended to bring about the objective. It requires constant management of resources, which is contrary, for example, to a society where free market forces alone determine the outcomes. Affirmative action programs are attractive only when they coincide with one's world view, with the idea that if certain factors are put in place, such as equality in government, education, and the workforce, it will indeed create a better society, a better world.

THE RIGHT TO WORK AND WORKER RIGHTS, AND MORE ABOUT FREEDOM

Freedom is a word often used to describe social policies (or the lack thereof) in the United States, and as already discussed, the word has diverse meanings. Certain types of freedoms are inherent to a democratic society and guaranteed by the state, such as the right to vote, freedom of speech and freedom of the press, and other legal freedoms including protection from criminal activity. Sometimes the line between what constitutes freedom and what does not becomes blurred, however. For example, should an individual have the freedom to marry any person he or she wishes, including those of the same sex? Or, to what extent should women have freedom to decide over their reproductive rights?

The line becomes even more blurred when we start talking about freedom from unwanted interference, for example, as in the separation of church and state and what constitutes freedom of religion versus freedom from religion. Defining freedom may be even more difficult when it comes to granting someone freedom to become whatever he or she wishes to become. Should women have freedom to be part of our military Special Forces, for instance? Or, to what extent should we grant the American Dream to every individual who resides in our country? Despite these difficulties with definition, one thing is clear. In order to exercise any kind of freedom, we need opportunity, and opportunity is often guided by our social and economic background. It is not enough to simply grant each individual a choice, if he or she is not also granted the means by which to realize the choice.

Since many freedoms require the support of the state, it is obvious that government is necessary in order to even begin realizing the freedoms that we typically view as inherent to a democratic society. Consider, for example, the so-called "right-to-work" states. A first, this sounds like a concept that increases the freedom of the individual. You can choose to take a job or you can choose not to. In either case, the choice is yours. You have the freedom. If the job in question is poorly regulated and offers starvation wages, the argument still holds true. You can choose to take the job or choose not to. Again, you have the freedom. In practicality, however, the right-to-work states do not increase the freedom of the individual, because the choice is often between accepting a job that pays starvation wages and taking no job at all. There is not much freedom in that kind of choice. Labor unions are an example of how the individual can increase his or her freedom through collective bargaining. Without the labor unions, the employee is at the mercy of the employer and has no choice but accepting a "take it or leave it" type of approach.[75]

More freedom for some thus means less freedom for others. Labor unions typically increase the freedom of the employee but decrease the freedom of the employer. When we talk about freedom, we thus attach different values to the word depending on where we stand on the social ladder. The important part to remember is that all members of society share the same values of right to "life, liberty, and the pursuit of happiness." When there are large inequalities, these values are restricted for large numbers of people. Reaching freedom is therefore about compromise, so that the largest number of people can benefit.

Olof Palme took a clear stand in favor of labor unions and worker rights. Having a job is a key component of a democratic socialist country, he argued, because being gainfully employed creates confidence and a feeling of inclusiveness, of being needed, and therefore fuels further initiative to move forward, grow, and contribute to making society even better. Self-sufficiency is crucial to any person's happiness. With respect to worker rights, however, there will always be conflicts of interest, no matter how hard we try to eradicate inequities and give everyone freedom to pursue happiness as he or she wishes. Once we acknowledge this fact, we can work to institute a system of checks and balances so that corporations and private industry do not take undue advantage of labor, and so that labor does not take undue advantage of the corporations and the welfare system. Politics is about making progress, making things better for the citizens of our country. Politics is a living force, and the aim is always to move toward a better future, not just for a select few of the powerful elite, but for society as a whole. Without checks on private industry, the workers will necessarily be exploited, and the environment will be harmed. This does not lead to a better world.

A healthy economy also requires healthy people. And healthy people require time to balance work and relaxation, family and time alone. The welfare of the people can be calculated on a cost/benefit basis. For instance, if people work too many hours or days without a break or sufficient vacation, or for low wages that require them to work two jobs to make ends meet, they will wear themselves out prematurely and ultimately cost society more in healthcare and other care related to aging. Furthermore, while business owners invest capital, labor invests their work and time, and therefore a large part of their lives. The idea is not to strive to do as little work as possible, but to achieve what one wishes to achieve and to have a say in work conditions that directly affect the employee. Since work must be done and we cannot get away from it, we should view it as central to a functioning society and not as a necessary evil. But the work environment must be inviting. Although the objective is to create work for all, it is equally important that we find the work satisfying and that it does not risk our health and well-being. Palme believed that public health was directly related to the conditions on the labor market.

As of the writing of this book, several businesses in Sweden are considering decreasing the workday from eight to six hours. Why? Because preliminary results indicate that working fewer hours increases morale and make workers more productive. For some companies in Sweden, the idea is not even that new. Toyota Services in Gothenburg, for example, "switched to a six-hour workday 13 years ago and reported higher profits and happier staff."[76] When employees are forced to work eight-hour days, they tend to mix in nonessential things, such as personal cell phone use and internet time, to combat fatigue and make the day bearable. This leads to less and not more productivity. Studies also show that a long workday makes it more difficult for families to function. There is more fatigue and less time for couples to spend with each other and with their kids. The shorter workday can be implemented successfully in business by limiting many unnecessary tasks, such as nonessential meetings and nonessential emails. While it is reported that workers in America would rather have more flexible work schedules than work fewer hours,[77] if truly given the choice, it would indeed be difficult to imagine that workers would turn down the six-hour day for the eight-hour day (it is assumed that monthly pay would remain the same), in return for the opportunity to surf the internet or visit with friends on Facebook while at work.

That said, in order to maintain a high standard of living, which leads to healthier and happier people with the individual freedom to rule their own lives and choose their own course, everybody must have an opportunity to be employed in a job that pays a living wage. No one should be forced to live below the poverty line or even close to it. When there are large pools of unemployed people, who are offered jobs on very poor terms, a cycle starts that leads to lower living standards, greater poverty, and greater difficulty to lift oneself out of poverty. Larger and larger parts of society will then come to suffer, and politics will have failed to achieve its objective of creating better conditions for the citizens.

Those taking a stand against certain welfare policies, such as unemployment benefits or social services including opportunities for education, tend to view the problem from the wrong perspective and see a causation where there is in fact only a correlation. For example, if education does not result in an unemployed person getting a job, we should not automatically assume that something is wrong with the welfare system and do away with the educational benefit. It may not be the benefit that is poor per se, but rather the fact that the labor market is saturated at the moment, causing unemployment among people also with higher education. As early as 1958, Palme argued that it was not possible to remain optimistic about the future with respect to technical developments, schools, energy, and roads, yet remain pessimistic when it came to solving the problem of social security and equality. Politicians preached about how they had confidence in the state's ability to grow with modern times, yet failed to mention the individual's need to grow and his or her hope in the future. Developments should therefore not merely focus on technical improvements, but also on individual developments.[78]

The problem is that those opposed to the sort of social reforms and government assistance that Palme suggested, while typically stating that there should be less government and more individual freedom, fail to think the thought to conclusion. Democratic socialism is about "government of the people, by the people, for the people," with government and individual necessarily intertwined. Without the individual, there would be no government. The government in turn has a responsibility to look out for the well-being of the individual. It is not the responsibility of family members or charities to help us rise from poverty, to support us during times of unemployment, to pay for our education, to care for us when we are sick or weak of old age. If this were the case, there would in fact be a middleman between us and the government, which would lead to less and not more individual freedom. When the government takes an active part in the well-being of the individual, we can leave behind the degradation that comes with having to ask others for help with life's necessities. The support the individual gets from the state contributes to increasing his or her freedom rather than taking it away.

Some say we should let the free market work it out, for fear that the government will limit the freedom of private ownership of business. But democratic socialism is not synonymous with taking away the right to ownership of private entities. We need private entities to fuel the economy. Public entities, by contrast, including national parks, healthcare, social security, and education, should not be privatized. In a truly democratic socialist nation, although industry is guided by market forces, social services such as education, healthcare, and financial protection when personal crisis strikes, are not. Industry is also regulated so that there are checks and balances, for example, on how to protect the environment.[79] Businesses in private ownership face rules that prevent those in power from trampling on the interests of the ordinary citizens and starting a downward social spiral of inequality, injustice, and ultimately poverty.

Welfare policy and individual freedom is thus not merely about the distribution of material resources. It is also about the distribution of power.[80] It is about the right of workers to organize, because it is only through the collective power of the labor unions that we can protect our working conditions and wages. Social welfare is not simply about the government handing out benefits to those in need, but about every citizen having the power to affect his or her situation, and the ability to act as a check and balance against the corporate interests of the super-wealthy, who can generally buy themselves powerful positions. It is a well-known fact in the United States that the powerful elite contributes enormous amounts of money to election campaigns, and can therefore buy the influence they need to sway the politicians in their favor. Elections are meant to be one vote per person, regardless of wealth. When Republican front runner and presidential candidate Mitt Romney declared in 2011 that "corporations are people, my friend,"[81] he simultaneously killed the idea of "government of the people, by the people, for the people." When the wealthy few sit on the power and make all the decisions, we will by nature create an unequal and socially unjust world that can hardly be called a democracy.

To be of true value, then, democratic socialism must rule in all aspects of life. Democratic principles cannot be halted, for example, the moment a person goes to work, as it would prove contradictory to expect people to partake in national elections, but give them no say in their day-to-day occupations.[82] This is where labor unions act as a democratic voice for the workers, and why they must exist in a democratic society. Without the existence of labor unions, democracy ends the moment one enters the workplace. As a graphic example, MBL or *medbestämmandelagen* (the law of codetermination) in Sweden regulates the relationship between employer and employee, and gives the employee the right to be part of decisions regarding his or her employment, the leadership of the company, and the day-to-day activities at work in general.

Furthermore, although we might find corruption among the officials running the labor unions, and might at times note how they benefit wrongfully by the monetary contributions of labor, this should not be taken as an indication that labor unions are by nature defective and should be eliminated. What we have is an issue of poor management. Successful democratic socialism is a balancing act between the individual and the collective, where the individual has a voice (through a vote). The collective cannot take actions that are not authorized by the individual through majority vote. Yes, there will by nature be friction, and neither side will be a hundred percent happy all the time.[83] But the purpose of politics as a living entity is never to be satisfied, because complete satisfaction leads to stagnation. At least some dissatisfaction will drive us to action away from stagnation and toward a better future.

THE HEALTHCARE DEBATE AND WHY THE MEANS-TEST SHOULD BE SCRAPPED

Olof Palme meant that in a just and progressive society, certain welfare programs, such as healthcare, unemployment benefits, and access to education must be universal to prove of value to every citizen, and should not be part of the free market. Contributing to these benefits should not be a choice left to the individual. Having both a private health insurance industry and a government run single-payer universal healthcare system to which all people pay taxes, for example, is not a viable solution, because it would result in higher taxes also for those choosing the private market and would thus lead to general discontent. Simultaneously, a for profit healthcare industry is not a viable solution, because the least privileged people in society, those who rely on welfare the most, cannot afford to pay into such a system and will thus be excluded. A reason why healthcare costs should not be market driven, is because the individual cannot choose whether to be healthy or sick, whether to use the services or not. Illness can strike anyone at anytime.

If social services, such as education, healthcare, childcare, and elderly care are items on the free market, it will permanently prevent large numbers of citizens from taking an active part in lifting the country from poverty and contributing to economic growth and a better future. In an ethical society, social services must be available to all people in proportion to their need and regardless of their income. Palme understood that need is not determined by profitability, but that every person's needs must be satisfied even when there is no financial gain. When all people have equal access to the use of social services, all people will also have a continued interest in that these services remain of high quality.[84] When the individual is no longer dependent on a job in order to get access to health insurance, the free market will also prosper, because he or she can take a job for which he is well suited, rather than a job that has a good health insurance plan. Both employer and employee will thus benefit.

Subsidized benefits for the poorer people of society, yet high premiums and deductibles for those who are determined as able to afford it, is an important focal point of the Affordable Care Act (popularly called Obamacare) in the United States. However, this type of means-test is also at the heart of a failing healthcare policy. As Palme said in a speech at Harvard University in 1984:

> If society's efforts are focused only on its weakest members through selective social policies largely based on "means-tests," taxpayers come to think in terms of "we" and "they." "We"—the better-off wage earners and the middle class—have to pay to the state, but get nothing in return. The ground is thus prepared for the disintegration of social solidarity.[85]

The best way to protect the weaker members of society is by including them "in programs that extend to all members of society," and not by giving them "special treatment."[86] This is why we need to think about the implications of policy decisions. It is not as simple as saying that a means-test sounds rational in theory, and should therefore be done. We must also consider how such a decision will ultimately affect society in the long run, including our vision of a more just world.

It is interesting to note that although Sven Palme, Olof Palme's paternal grandfather and an officer who was friendly toward the military, had deviated from his earlier social democratic views and drifted toward the right on the political spectrum, he was still liberal with respect to healthcare and social insurance for all, and may have influenced the younger Palme's views. At a time when many people looked to Germany, who relied on a social insurance model that only covered the wage earner, Sven Palme strove for universal insurance that included every citizen. As an insurance worker, he had firsthand knowledge of how those who needed insurance the most; namely, the sick, incapacitated, or unemployed, were also those who were least likely to be able to afford it, and least likely to be able to protect themselves against even worse conditions. He understood that the state and the individual were mutually dependent on one another and could not be treated as separate entities.[87]

In a Special to CNN in 2012, House Minority Leader Nancy Pelosi reminded us of President Lyndon Johnson's words the day he signed the Medicare bill:

> No longer will older Americans be denied the healing miracle of modern medicine. No longer will illness crush and destroy the savings that they have so carefully put away over a lifetime so that they might enjoy dignity in their later years. No longer will young families see their own incomes, and their own hopes, eaten away simply because they are carrying out their deep moral obligations to their parents, and to their uncles, and their aunts. And no longer will this nation refuse the hand of

justice to those who have given a lifetime of service and wisdom and labor to the progress of this progressive country.[88]

Humans have a right to education, healthcare, and social security. The difference is that in a democratic socialist country, this is seen as a universal right and not a privilege based on financial status. There is no means-test. Rich and poor alike have equal access to these benefits. Lyndon Johnson signed the Medicare bill in 1965. We may have come a long way with respect to healthcare for the elderly. But when it comes to healthcare for all, young as well as old, we still have a very long way to go.

EDUCATION IS NOT A SNOBBISH WORD

The type of social democracy that was prevalent in Sweden in 1944 toward the end of World War II, when Olof Palme was a young man who had just finished his basic schooling, spoke of the coming peace and how the future would look. In the years between the World Wars, there had been a huge economic recession and period of unemployment, which, some claimed, was likely the result of too liberal views on the economic market. In order to avoid another crisis, the new social democracy must therefore include more government controls and an actively organized welfare society with plenty of educational opportunities, as this would guard against mass unemployment that would tempt young men to turn to extremist and totalitarian viewpoints.[89]

Palme believed that education was one of the more important factors that contributed to social and gender equality. But in order to achieve the objective, everybody must have access to the same education. Everybody might not achieve the same level of education or score as high as others, but everybody should have the same start in life through access to the same educational standards. In the early 1950s, there was thus a push in Sweden for access to higher education for all, regardless of one's rung on the socioeconomic ladder. The ability to choose the road that resonated best with one's interests was the difference between a democracy and a dictatorship, it was argued. But it also meant that those who could not afford it must have access to and be granted higher academic education. The country would reach elite status on the international level only if more youth had opportunity to continue their studies.[90]

In the early 1960s, there was continued serious debate about how to make higher education available to all who desired it. The obvious solution was to subsidize education for those who had financial need, while letting those who were better off finance their own education. But Swedish democratic socialism had already at that time distanced itself from the means-test, which was viewed as condescending to the individual by causing a natural rift between rich and poor. Subsidies should become a universal right, it was argued. It was in part about preventing a situation where young but grownup men and women would end up dependent on their parents' ability and willingness to pay, and in part about preventing situations where women who wished to study would be denied a state subsidy because their husband's income was too high. The principle that all students, regardless of income or background, would have equal access to state financed education proved robust later, when educational opportunities were broadened to encompass large numbers of students.[91]

While Palme supported these policies whole-heartedly, he was less fond of those who had achieved higher status as a result of their privileged financial situations, and now, with state financing for education on the table, worried about protecting their elite status.[92] The idea was not to drag down those who were well off to the level of the poor, however, but to raise everybody higher. The problem inherent to a heavily divided class society is that those better off tend to get little pleasure from their success, unless there are also poor people against whom they can measure themselves. What defines rich is often the relationship we experience toward the poor. As a result, when society lacks measures for equality, the privileged classes will increase their own richness at the expense of the poor, and society will become even more divided. This breeds animosity and restlessness between social groups, also when the purpose of equality is to harmonize society rather than split it.

As discussed repeatedly, democratic socialism is about giving people power over their own lives. It is not about taking away freedom by "requiring everybody to be the same," as those opposed to the concept suggest, but about giving people greater freedom to live as they wish within the law. Those with unequal educational, financial, and social opportunities will naturally have unequal opportunities to seek the path they desire. But we all face similar challenges from cradle to grave, even if these challenges will manifest themselves in different ways. In a speech at Harvard University in 1984, Palme said:

> During the course of life, we all meet the same challenges: to grow up and be educated; to find playmates and friends; to prepare ourselves for our different roles in adult life and make our own living; to find somewhere to live and make it into a home; to form a family and bring up children; to keep healthy throughout life and cope with illness and other misfortunes that may beset us; to secure a decent living and preserve our dignity for the inevitable frailty of old age; to live as free citizens, equal with other members of society; and to take a share in being responsible for the common good.[93]

A well-developed social welfare state, where everybody can get an education, gainful employment, and healthcare, promotes the freedom of the individual and gives him or her an opportunity to pursue his dreams while young and healthy. But it does not end there. Social welfare and educational assistance also benefit society and the country as a whole, which is why it should not be viewed merely as welfare for the individual, or an entitlement that is given away on demand. Social and educational benefits are good for the nation, because an individual who is educated and healthy can make a bigger contribution to society and the growth of the economy. An uneducated or sick person can hardly be expected to contribute greatly by working and paying taxes. For contrasting purposes, note that in 2012, Republican presidential candidate Rick Santorum called President Barack Obama a "snob" for suggesting that everybody in the United States should be encouraged to go to college.[94]

Even when the goal of democratic socialism is to increase the freedom of the individual, so that he or she can live his or her chosen path to the fullest, we must be cautions of the idea that being free to choose which educational institution to attend: public, private, or homeschooling, does not necessarily increase individual freedom, unless we have certain checks and balances in place. What generally happens when we enact these sorts of choices is that those who are better off will require that their children have access to private schools and elite institutions, while those less well off will still lack a choice. Individual freedom often becomes the freedom only of the strong and the wealthy to utilize the resources that society has built collectively during the course of many decades or even centuries. Even the term citizenship is considered by many democratic socialists a right-leaning term that is not fully inclusive, and many find it more proper to talk about people and society rather than citizens.

HIGH TAXES, IMMIGRATION, AND
FOREIGN POLICY CRITICS

To reach success with democratic socialism, the system must be managed. If we let individual freedom run wild, the strong and wealthy will oppress the weak and poor. On the other hand, if we let collective freedom run wild, individual freedom will be severely limited by the group. Neither is a good world to live in. Part of the difficulty inherent to striking a proper political balance, is that human beings are simultaneously individuals who want full freedom to determine the course of their lives without government interference, and social animals who are part of civilization and therefore part of a greater collective.[95] In order to prove successful, any system of government needs oversight and transparency. To understand this better, let us look at an example from Sweden a few decades ago, related to the much debated high taxation we generally hear about in democratic socialist countries.

In the late 1970s, the Swedish population was naturally not happy about paying high taxes. But the root of their unhappiness was not high taxes per se, since everybody knew that taxes were necessary for the successful continuation of the welfare state. The root of the problem was the large bureaucracy that surrounded the tax code and the fact that many loopholes existed almost solely for the benefit of the wealthy. People were also unhappy because the Social Democratic Workers' Party had held power for forty-three years, and had in many people's eyes become arrogant. An investigation into the matter indicated that the Swedes in general trusted the state to do the right thing, more so than they trusted individual entities on both sides on the political spectrum, such as labor unions and big business. The whole idea of a strong state was to increase individual freedom by giving all people equal opportunity to live the life they desired. In election after election, the Swedish people had chosen a neutral entity, such as the state, as the holder of collective power, and avoided giving power to various lobbies or organizations of special interest.[96]

However, four decades of social democratic rule had made the government stale. As a result of this general unhappiness with the status quo, the right-leaning parties won the election in 1976. Various foreign newspapers such as the *Wall Street Journal* wrote that the Swedes had finally kicked out the socialists, and the French *Le Monde* explained that the Swedes had said no to the Social Democratic Workers' Party because it was monolithic and its views no longer seemed plausible. The British *Financial Times* came closer to the truth, however, when it wrote that the Swedish model endured; it was only in the shop for repair. The right-leaning government had only won a marginal victory, and most policies in Sweden would remain unchanged. In fact, the new prime minister Thorbjörn Fälldin explained that solidarity would survive and the elderly, sick, and weak could count on continued support from the state. Olof Palme, in turn, explained that the Social Democratic Workers' Party would not become a brake to progress by opposing every idea the right-leaning government proposed. Instead, he promised to work in a bipartisan way and help the new prime minister guide the country in the proper direction.[97] This reasoning stands in stark contrast, for example, to when President Barack Obama won the presidency in the United States, and the Republican Party became known as "the party of 'no.'" Several members of the GOP swore that their primary goal was to make President Obama a one-term president. They swore to oppose him no matter what he suggested; in short, if he was for it, they were against it.[98]

What pulled Palme toward democratic socialism, however, was not a belief in high taxation and government control of business, and certainly not the status quo, but a belief in equality and the modernization of society. The goal was to mow down the barriers that stood in the way of the people to develop their true personalities and follow the course in life that they felt was their calling. He wanted to break free from the conservative mindset that emphasized stable norms, strong family values, free market economy, clear boundaries between classes, and well-defined gender roles.[99] In an interview with British historian Perry Anderson, Palme explained that social welfare was not merely about preventing poverty, but about guaranteeing the citizens a good standard of living.[100] It was thus more about the future than the past, and about giving people greater ability to realize their dreams by tearing down the old hierarchical system and democratize education so that, with the assistance of the state, individuals could gain greater control over their lives.[101] He was opposed to any belief in a predetermined destiny, as in the idea that if one did nothing, democratic socialism (or the free market, for that matter) would win in the end. Dynamic interaction with the people was needed in order to reach the objectives.

However, while all of Palme's political life was dedicated to making society fully inclusive of all people, his well-meaning ideas did not always materialize. An example may be the assimilation of immigrants. In the mid-twentieth century, when the policies of the Swedish welfare state were growing, Sweden was largely a homogenous country. Today, with a large immigrant population, society has become more segregated. Immigrants are often placed in subordinate positions on the labor market, sometimes because of language difficulties, but often because of clear discriminatory actions. As a result, they typically earn less than the average Swede, and therefore cannot afford to live in the more attractive areas with the best housing opportunities. The fact that large numbers of immigrant populations end up "segregated" (not necessarily by choice by either side, but as a result of cultural factors), leads to that more children grow up in conditions that border on poverty and have difficulty achieving the same level of education as the better off native Swedish children. This naturally leads us back to greater gaps in earning potential and greater inequality in general.[102]

Furthermore, while most people in the mid-twentieth century came from nearly the same social and geographic background, and there was huge support for a welfare state where everybody would benefit almost equally, today, with large numbers of immigrants living close to poverty, these will naturally draw the greatest benefits from social programs. The result is that the native Swedes feel excluded. Since those better off do not want to carry the full burden of paying for these benefits, support for the welfare state has declined.[103] This is not synonymous with saying that the whole idea of democratic socialism that worked so well within Sweden fifty years ago should be scrapped, however. Instead, we should acknowledge that the country faces new challenges in a new century. New solutions to these problems should be sought in a way that will continue to drive the country forward on the road to improvements for all.

To approach the immigration problem from a slightly different perspective and consider whether Palme was correct in opening Sweden to large immigrant populations, let us consider a few different viewpoints. Michael Scheuer is a former CIA intelligence officer and foreign policy critic. According to him:

> Western and U.S. governments have destabilized their own societies by basically having no effective immigration controls for more than thirty years. The negative impact of this failure is especially strong in countries that historically have been ethnically and linguistically homogenous, countries like Norway [Norway is Sweden's closest neighbor and entertains similar political views]. Western governments have assumed and declared that all newcomers both want to and can be assimilated into the indigenous culture. This has been and is a false and an ahistorical assumption; the publicly announced position of some Muslim leaders in Europe and North America, for example, is that they have no intention of assimilating. Most countries in the West have any number of citizens who believe uncontrolled immigration is ruining their society and that the government takes the side of newcomers over people whose families have lived and helped build a particular country for many generations. The result in Oslo [the capital of Norway] was violence, as it will be elsewhere, including in the United States.[104]

We might also want to look at how democracy is considered by foreign policy critics. Retired United States Army lieutenant colonel and media commentator Ralph Peters, for instance, takes this view:

> Historically, democracy has worked well in two types of environment. First, it works in homogeneous nations, such as Sweden, where there are no serious ethnic or religious differences and the citizen allocates his or her vote based upon individual concerns. The second situation in which democracy works well is a state—such as the United States—whose populace is so diverse in ethnic origin, religion, and race that no single group can dominate all the others at the national level. Parties must build complex, shifting coalitions and can't permanently exclude anyone. Both forms of democracy work well, although the more complex U.S. version generates greater social and cultural dynamism—more forward motion—while the European model plays it safe, elevating group welfare over individual opportunity.[105]

In Peters' case, while the perspective is interesting, it is not clear in what ways the Swedish people have less individual opportunity because of the group welfare system. As stated repeatedly throughout this book, from our perspective it is democratic socialism per se that has contributed to greater, not less, individual opportunity and freedom by avoiding dependence on family or church or other charitable organizations when crisis strikes, and by avoiding dependence on employment for access to truly affordable healthcare.

Thomas Peterffy, a Hungarian-born American entrepreneur, is yet a critic of socialism. In support of the Republican Party in the United States, he published an advertisement on YouTube stating that, despite the fact that he could not speak English when he immigrated to the United States in 1956, he still fulfilled the American Dream, not with help from a welfare system, but with hard work and dedication:

> I grew up in a socialist country, and I have seen what that does to people. There is no hope, no freedom, no pride in achievement . . . America's wealth comes from the efforts of people striving for success. Take away their incentive by badmouthing success, and you take away the wealth that helps us take care of the needy. Yes, in socialism the rich will be poorer. But the poor will also be poorer. People will lose interest in really working hard and creating jobs. I think this is a very slippery slope. It seems like people don't learn from the past.[106]

Thomas Peterffy correctly states that we do not learn from the past. But he fails to mention that the reason why is because no two historical situations are the same. The Hungary where he grew up during and after World War II is not the United States of today, and certainly not post-World War II Sweden. There is no Soviet occupation in the United States (and not in Sweden) and never was. (In fact, there is no Soviet

Union!) Furthermore, modern democratic socialism is not even remotely related to communism. This is why we must be careful with anecdotal stories like this. One of the replies to Peterffy's YouTube advertisement noted the following:

> This absurd equation of Obama's administration with the Soviet occupation of Hungary is no more accurate than comparing Romney and the GOP to fascists. This ad is a cynical manipulation of the facts and opportunistic exploitation of the notion of the American Dream. The whole idea that a centrist democrat could lead us into Soviet-style communism is asinine, and it cheapens the very real struggles and dangers people faced during Hungary's communist era![107]

What we should learn from these critics of democratic socialism is that both praise and criticism must be placed in context, if it is to have value and become a guiding light for future action.

NO ONE IS AN ISLAND

When Olof Palme became prime minister of Sweden in 1969, many countries including the United States commented on the election, and some expressed that the Swedes, this careful and quiet people who typically chose not to make waves and valued compromise and teamwork, had suddenly acquired a leader who had international ambitions and was ready to fight.[108] Palme had the ability to move things to action, which is a reason why he was viewed as such an astounding person and politician. He was an optimist and held the steadfast belief that it was possible to change the world for the better.

While he succeeded with political reforms on home turf, his reputation was greatest on the international scene, and not until his death, when leaders and commoners from all corners of the globe voiced their sorrow in media interviews, did the Swedish people realize the enormous impact Palme had had on the oppressed countries of the world. When Palme died, for a moment all people shared a common bond. They were all human, regardless of whether they were young punk kids in Sweden, single mothers, lower class laborers, elderly men or women struggling to make ends meet, immigrants who barely spoke the Swedish language, or politicians from the opposition party.

How did he gain such international fame? Palme's mother came to Sweden from Latvia as a refugee during World War I, which might have opened his eyes toward refugees and immigrants. Simultaneously, he realized that refugees and immigrants had a tough time adjusting to Swedish society, in part because the Swedish people were not necessarily "easy" to get to know and live with side-by-side.[109] Palme was also opposed to war in any form or way, because he viewed it as one of the greatest threats to the welfare and prosperity of mankind. Poorer countries naturally fared badly when engaged in war, but even richer nations could easily be decimated by the toll that war took in human lives and resources.

At the conclusion of World War II, Palme believed that Sweden should remain neutral and not be part of any large alliances. Sweden should remain part of the Marshal Plan, but for the sole purpose of fighting hunger, poverty, and hopelessness, and not for taking a political stand at the side of the United States. While largely pro-American and embracing American values, not the least because the United States contributed with large sums of money to rebuild the war ravaged Europe, Palme was simultaneously cautiously aware of the fact that a pro-American attitude among the younger population could lead to the United States eventually attempting to use European and Swedish youth as tools to further their own foreign policy.[110]

Although Palme detested war in any form and was against small nations becoming engaged in the complicated alliances of the superpowers, he believed in a strong defense establishment for the small country of Sweden. A strong defense would help neutral Sweden gain credibility and help it defend itself against possible outside aggression without calling for help from allies.[111] In 1977, Palme also noted in a lecture at Stanford University that the arms race between rich nations was out of proportion, and the amount of money invested in defense did not result in a proportionally large increase in material security for the citizens. The money and effort spent on building up the military might of Western nations could be much better spent on projects that directly led to increased happiness for the citizens.[112]

Palme thus had vision. He was not merely stating that he was a proponent of peace. He fully recognized the need to invest in the citizens and the infrastructure of his country. He recognized that large economic and social differences between people naturally leads to unrest. He argued that when we find a way out of poverty, when we see improvements at home and get our individual dreams realized, we are also contributing to stabilizing society and making a long lasting peace possible. Large spending on military developments will then no longer be needed.

When asked in an interview with British journalist David Frost in 1969 what sorts of people he admired, Palme said that he admired those "who are steadfast in their basic ideology and prepared to do very hard, and tiresome, and tedious work." On the international scene, he found the idea naïve that impoverished nations could become democratic. Such a belief merely reflected a desire of wealthy nations, like Sweden and the United States, to avoid taking responsibility for the true needs of these poorer countries. He confessed that his ideas on foreign aid were "far too easy [underdeveloped] in the beginning," and that it is not possible to simply bring people to Sweden and educate them in order to help the poor countries lift themselves from poverty.[113]

Regarding the struggle between Israel and Palestine, he stood on the side of the Palestinians, but he also openly recognized Israel's right to exist. The difference was that he believed it absolutely necessary for peace, and also a fundamental right of the Palestinians, to have a state of their own and be in control of their future. He heavily opposed Israeli expansion and settlements on the West Bank, as expressed in a speech in 1983.[114] He further said that he did not "wish to be an advocate for armed struggle," but that he understood it: "When people who are seeking peaceful progression meet only brutal oppression, they will naturally embrace violence—if only in self-defense."[115]

Although he was heavily opposed to war in any form, from the United States involvement in Vietnam to the racial struggles in South Africa, Palme asserted that there is a difference between anti-Americanism and a strong criticism of American foreign policy. His anti-war views regarding Vietnam were, after all, held by large numbers of Americans as well. His belief, even though he spoke against the United States actions in Vietnam, was that the United States otherwise was an ally of Sweden. But the basic values of democratic socialism mandated that Sweden stand on the side of the oppressed peoples in the world, on the side of the poor, and against the oppressors and those who wish to dominate and rule over others. Although Sweden remained neutral in World War II, and as a result acquired a poor reputation among those who viewed Sweden as cowardly for not taking a firm stance on the side of the allies, the word neutrality and the refusal to stand by the United States now gained a slightly more positive meaning which, during the Vietnam War, became associated with solidarity, autonomy, and courage.[116]

One should call things by their proper names, said Palme when the United States bombed Hanoi in Vietnam during Christmas 1972. The United States were torturing a population for the purpose of demonstrating power and superiority, he claimed. When asked if he considered Richard Nixon's actions in Vietnam equal in principle to what Hitler had done to the Jews in World War II, Palme answered that they were equal in the sense of violence toward the individual; that it was not the politicians (Hitler and Nixon) he compared, but the meaningless violence against the individual, as when violence ceases to accomplish anything of importance.

Henry Kissinger expressed concern and found the Swedish attitude toward the United States "insensitive." He believed that Palme had in fact compared the United States to the Nazis, which he thought doubly problematic considering the fact that the United States had fought against the Nazis in World War II. Other Americans claimed that Sweden prided itself on a policy of neutrality, but was in fact not neutral, as evidenced by the statements made by Palme. As a result of these statements, the United States withdrew its ambassador to Sweden, and Sweden also withdrew its senior envoy from Washington for two years. When the Vietnam War ended in 1975, Palme said that we should not believe that Vietnam would even remotely resemble a Western democracy any time soon. What was important instead was to stop the sufferings of the people, to make sure that children could get food and clothes, and that all could have a place to live and work.[117]

With respect to defense and military intervention, of particular importance may be that Palme noted how we tend to distort the definition of defense in order to justify taking offensive action against other countries that pose no immediate threat to our own. In short, he referred to this as the "law of the jungle" where the strongest dominate the weakest,[118] or to quote ancient Athenian historian and political philosopher Thucydides: "Right, as the world goes, is only in question between equals in power, while the strong do what they can and the weak suffer what they must."[119] Although the definition of what is necessary can be debated, an unnecessary war often results in a Pyrrhic victory, or one of great loss even for the victors. This is why we still feel the effects of the

Vietnam War, and certainly the effects of our intervention in Iraq in the twenty-first century and the turmoil it started, even though human casualties for the United States in Iraq were not on the astronomical scale.

Regarding apartheid, Palme viewed it as "a unique form of evil, a form of tyranny that brands a person from birth because of the color of his or her skin."[120] Palme spearheaded Sweden's contributions of state funds to the African National Congress and to democratic movements in other African countries as early as the 1960s.

When news spread of Olof Palme's death in 1986, Sweden reacted with shock and disbelief. "This is the worst thing that could have happened to Sweden," said a passerby interviewed on the street by the murder site in Stockholm. Another man confessed that the reason why he had come to the murder site was to see with his own eyes that what the media was saying was really the truth, because he "could not believe it at first." Olof Palme left behind a great vacuum in Swedish and international politics. As Swedish journalist Dieter Strand commented, Palme's quickness of mind, his perspective on both domestic and international issues, would be greatly missed and not easily replaced.[121] Said Oliver Tambo, South African anti-apartheid politician and president of the African National Congress, after the murder of Olof Palme:

> We have come to know him [Olof Palme] not only as a leader of the Swedish people and an international statesman, but also as one of us, a fellow combatant . . . From Vietnam to Nicaragua, from El Salvador to Palestine, from Sahara to South Africa, across the face of the globe, the flags hang

limp and half mast in loving memory of this giant of justice, who had become a citizen of the world, a brother and a comrade to all who are downtrodden.[122]

CAN WE SUCCEED?

Olof Palme's Sweden was way ahead of the times. Thirty years after Palme's death, when it comes to humanitarian questions and the basic rights of the people, the United States has not even begun to catch up. But to what extent was Palme correct in promoting democratic socialist ideals in both domestic and foreign policy? Can his policies be transferred to countries such as the United States today and prove successful?

Although it is easy to agree in principle with democratic socialist ideals; for example, that everybody should have equal access to education and paid vacation and sick days from work, the problem is the fear many of us have that such policies will lead to lazy workers. The argument is that the welfare state will eventually lower the more ambitious and harder workers to the level of those who deliberately take advantage of the system, and thus start a downward spiral that will degrade all of society. Naturally, nobody wants to support those who call in sick to work every Monday, simply because they suffer a hangover from the weekend's partying. Naturally, we also oppose giving up our university place to someone who has not applied himself and worked as hard to earn good grades. Hard work should be rewarded, and those who deserve an A should get an A, while those who deserve an F should get an F. The basic idea, however, is not to lower the upper classes to the level of the lower classes, but to raise the lower classes higher in order to give all of society a boost.

Those opposed to democratic socialism further argue that when the disparities between rich and poor are eradicated, the will to work hard will disappear and society will stagnate because no one will feel justly compensated for their hard work. Those who take the democratic socialist stance, by contrast, argue that the best society grows from creativity and the ability to develop each person's unique strengths, and that large disparities between rich and poor hamper this ability in the less fortunate, who do not have the same access to education and the job market, who must work longer hours merely to make ends meet, and whose health is often failing prematurely due to lack of adequate healthcare and decent living arrangements. While those to the right on the political spectrum argue that democratic socialism destroys individualism and initiative, the democratic socialists argue the opposite: that it is the greater access to government institutions such as education and healthcare, decent housing, etc. that allows the individual to flourish and, in fact, gives him or her greater freedom to pursue individual initiatives.

The crux of the matter, and which is seldom if ever confronted openly in political debates in the United States, is that in order for the democratic socialist argument to retain its validity, the universal benefits of the welfare state, such as education and healthcare, must in fact be universal and given equally to all, rich and poor, without a means-test intended only to help the needy. Why no means-test? Because a means-test that determines who gets a grant for college, or who gets government assistance with healthcare expenses, may not only kill the initiative to work hard, but will unequivocally be divisive. Hardworking men and women naturally do not want to subsidize those who do not work, while drawing no benefit from it. But if the benefit applies equally to all regardless of income, it will not promote laziness or divisiveness. The poor should not be given special benefits, but should be included in programs that are extended equally to all people, regardless of income or social status.[123] This is the part that the Democratic Party in the United States seems to have missed. Hillary Clinton, for example, calls on families "to do their part," and said during a recent appearance before the Des Moines Register's editorial board that she is "not going to give, you know, free college to wealthy kids."[124]

A greater problem, however, might be that even if we agree in principle with the so-called "Swedish model" of democratic socialism presented in this book, no political system or ideology can be transported flawlessly to another country. Any model for social reform must be based on the specific history of the people and country in question. Since Sweden and the United States have vastly different pasts, it is not possible to transport the Swedish model to the United States, without also transporting the whole history of Sweden; the whole country, in fact, which naturally cannot be done. It takes time and vision to build a system of democratic socialism that suits the mentality of the people. Modern democratic socialism in Sweden has been developed over a period of decades, but is based on the history of centuries. It is therefore not possible to take a great leap overnight, for example, from a political reality that guarantees no one access to health insurance, as we so recently had in the United States, to a single-payer universal healthcare system, as proposed by Vermont senator and self-proclaimed socialist Bernie Sanders. Successful reform takes time to implement, even if we agree in principle that reform is needed.

Although we may not take the socialist stance easily, at the very least, it behooves us to listen to what the proponents of democratic socialism have to say, particularly in an election year. In order to know how to proceed, we must educate ourselves about its meaning, and understand that democratic socialism is not a throwback to the Soviet Union or communist China, but a progressive outlook that leads to a new and better world. According to Bernie Sanders, "socialist" is often misunderstood, and must be placed in proper context; for example, by considering the fact that the Scandinavian countries—Sweden, Denmark, Norway—have democratic socialist governments and view healthcare as a "right of all people." Tuition is free in those countries at a time when so many young people in the United States cannot afford to go to college. The democratic socialist countries also have "excellent childcare [and] strong retirement benefits." They are also strong on protecting the environment. As Sanders states, once people understand that "in those countries, governments are working for the middle class rather than the billionaire class," we will also understand that "socialist" is not a dirty word.[125]

When Bernie Sanders, who follows the Scandinavian model of democratic socialism, spoke at Liberty University on September 14, 2015, he focused on issues of morality, justice, and human decency. He stated repeatedly that it is hard to make the case that the United States, the wealthiest country in the history of the world, is a "just society, or anything resembling a just society today." A the same time that millions of Americans, including children, starve and cannot afford to go to the doctor when sick, a handful of billionaires have more money than they will know what to do with for generations to come. Sanders argued that "there is no justice when so few have so much and so many so little."[126]

In the United States, some 45 million Americans live in poverty. In Sander's view, this is not justice. It is a "rigged economy, designed by the wealthiest people in this country to benefit the wealthiest people in this country at the expense of everybody else." Americans of all stripes love to talk about family values. But the United States is the only Western country where mothers must separate from their newborn babies within a week or two of giving birth, because there is not paid maternity leave. In all other modern countries on earth, new mothers get at least some paid leave after giving birth, so that they can bond with their babies and provide the care that is so desperately needed in the first months of a new life. Something is morally wrong, Sanders said, quoting Pope Francis, when money rules rather than serves.[127]

Can a socialist like Bernie Sanders succeed in America? Sander's agenda includes "single-payer healthcare, free tuition at public colleges, affordable daycare, billions more for Social Security, [and] higher taxes on the wealthy, [in addition to] the most dramatic expansion of government in three generations." To the majority of the lower and middle classes, this might sound extraordinarily inviting. But according to some political analysts, Sanders is also a "brusque and inflexible loner," an outsider who lacks the support he needs from his own party, and probably does not have a great chance of proving effective at implementing the changes he proposes, should he by chance be elected the next president of the United States. In fact, "Sander's most recent bills—promoting free college and universal healthcare—drew zero Democratic cosponsors."[128]

The foregoing is testament to that we must live in our time and culture, and within the history of our country. While Olof Palme was an insider and a man with whom the masses identified, Bernie Sanders is an outsider who does not follow the mainstream parties in the United States. While Olof Palme was admired for standing by his ideals, Bernie Sanders is viewed as a loner who is incapable of change. In order for Bernie Sanders to prove successful in the United States, we must enact some major cultural changes, which will prove exceedingly difficult and certainly take a very long time.

How we interpret democratic socialism, then, depends on our times, country, culture, and circumstances. When we talk about democratic socialism in the United States, many people abhor the idea because they do not understand it and equate it to the communist movements of China and the former Soviet Union. They do not understand that no one in the modern Western world would strive for anything that even remotely resembled those regimes. When deciding which political approach works best, we must place it in context and question what types of conditions we ultimately seek for our people today. We cannot base it solely on examples from outdated times and different cultures, and we must be aware and cautious of this trap.

So, where does this leave us? The American Dream is open to all in theory; all have the opportunity to partake in it or at least chase it, no matter what our background, but the reality is less bright. All people do in fact not have the opportunity to take advantage of the American Dream. Hard work does not lead to success for all. Some people's social inheritance will always produce a hindrance no matter how hard they work or try to break free. When we talk about "freedom" in America, it is not a freedom that all can reach. When we speak of less government, we should remember that the type of freedom we get through less government, also leads to greater uncertainty and more difficulties for a large part of our population. This is the reason why freedom is a "prison sentence" (figuratively speaking) to some, while others consider it a "god-given right." The idea of democratic socialism is to create security for the people. Not until we can trust in our government and the political path we are taking, can we set aside worries about the future.

With the foregoing in mind, avoiding stagnation requires a clear desire for progress. While it may prove honorable to defend already enacted laws that in the past have served us well, continuing on the same "good ol' path" is not good enough. Maintaining the status quo, or what is commonly termed conservatism or resistance to change, is not what good politics is about. We must retest political methods in order to stay with changing times and the wishes of the people. In a civilized country, we depend on each other. Although we may choose different roads, all of us still have a road, and all of us still need the help and association of others. As citizens of our country, we are necessarily influenced by how society functions. Only when the power is more equally distributed will we have the opportunity to develop our individualism according to our wishes.

The subtitle of the book you have nearly finished reading is *New Socialism for a Modern World*. But why "new"? As has been stated repeatedly, politics is a living entity, and when we refuse to modernize and go with the times and the tides, we will eventually wither and die. Democratic socialism is also not a throwback to the communism of the former Soviet Union. The United States has a long history of anti-communist views, to the point that we often do not dare to discuss socialism in earnest for fear of being branded a communist. But the time of Cold War communism is past, and we need to move forward. But how? Instead of expecting the United States to model itself after Sweden, we should consider what is truly important to the future of our country and people: to minimize suffering on all levels and give people an equal chance to prosper; to help those in need, without pulling down or throwing dirt on those who are successful. All should have a decent place to live in security, a job that pays a livable wage, a chance for higher education, and access to truly affordable healthcare without fear of being financially ruined when tragedy strikes. So, no, it is not the socialism that Sweden lived for in the 1960s or 1970s that we should strive to emulate. Instead, we should ask what we want from our society today and tomorrow, and how we can achieve it—but always with the masses in mind, and not merely for the benefit of the millionaires and billionaires.

Is ideology always bad, then? Is pragmatism always good? As has been said, "History is not necessarily progressive in its outcomes."[129] If we want to change the world, we must believe that the world can be changed. We must stand by our vision until the objectives are achieved. Our strife must resonate with the direction the rest of the developed world is moving. Democratic socialism is not just about you, the individual, but about all people who have inherited the world in which we live. We can never go back, we must always move forward, and when we do, we must think about what is best for us, all of us, as in "We the People." Democratic socialism is thus about your journey, but it is also about mine.

AFTERWORD

When Olof Palme was asked during an interview in his younger years how he would like to be remembered, and what he would like his obituary to say, he said it was a thought he had never entertained. He further stated that it was not something he desired to think about, because "the moment people begin to think of their obituaries, they start to be scared, they don't dare to do things, and they lose their vitality," and since "we are doomed to be on this earth, we should try to make life as decent as possible. That is simply the very basis of my political ideology."[130]

When debating politics and political ideologies, it is primarily the idea and not the person or messenger of the idea that should be debated, critiqued, or criticized. But we also cannot discount the messenger entirely. Olof Palme was by some considered the greatest political genius Sweden had ever had. Although it was not Palme who started the social democratic movement, he clarified it in terms the people could understand. He defined what it meant to be a social democrat or democratic socialist, as he called himself. He was proud of the definition and not only demonstrated superb knowledge of the term through captivating speeches and powerful action, but also lived his personal life according to the ideal, never deviating from it despite his upper class background. "It was impossible to ignore his questions," said Henry Kissinger after Palme was murdered in 1986. "So for all whose lives Olof Palme touched, the world has become a far lonelier place."[131]

Anna Lindh, chairman and speaker for SSU (Sveriges Socialdemokratiska Ungdomsförbund or Swedish Social Democratic Youth League) concurred and said that "our gratitude toward you [Olof Palme] shall not stagnate at that which has been, but be directed toward the future, for a person can be murdered, but not the ideas. Your ideas continue to live through us. We shall continue your struggle to the best of our ability, the struggle for peace and international solidarity, the struggle for an open and free Sweden without racism and animosity toward foreigners. This is our duty."[132]

The most important task of a politician is the ability to listen to the people, to the masses, to the commoners. Politicians want power, because it is through power that they accomplish their objectives. But the power they enjoy must be used to the benefit of the people, or it is of little value.[133] The role of a politician, or a party leader, or a president therefore comes with tremendous responsibilities. When Olof Palme died, Sweden had reached far regarding social welfare, equality, and human rights. Palme was there from the beginning and laid the foundation for these ideas.

So, what about the rest of us? Well, we can start on our path forward by remembering that nations are designed to grow for our benefit, for us, as in "We the People," with government "of the people, by the people, for the people." No nation is by nature a straitjacket that must control our destiny for time and eternity. Or, as alluded to so eloquently by Victor Hugo in *Les Misérables*:

> If we take Waterloo from Wellington and Blucher, do we thereby deprive England and Germany of anything? No. Neither that illustrious England nor that august Germany enter into the problem of Waterloo. Thank Heaven, nations are great, independently of the lugubrious

feats of the sword. Neither England, nor Germany, nor France is contained in a scabbard.[134]

APPENDIX

NOT IKEA SIMPLE:
WHY SWEDEN RECOGNIZED PALESTINE

On October 30, 2014, Sweden officially recognized the Palestinian state. In response, Israel's Minister of Foreign Affairs Avigdor Lieberman expressed that the conflict between Israel and Palestine is not simple, like a self-assembled piece of IKEA furniture. Sweden's Minister of Foreign Affairs Margot Wallström replied that she would be "happy to send Israel FM Lieberman an IKEA flat pack to assemble. He'll see it requires a partner, cooperation, and a good manual."[135] This brief appendix examines the perspectives of several parties, including Sweden, Israel, Palestine, and the other Nordic countries, and is intended as a starting point for those desiring to debate left-leaning foreign policy views.

On October 2, 2014, based on the results of a recent election, Sweden chose a new left-leaning democratic socialist government, with Prime Minister Stefan Löfven at the helm. On October 30, 2014, Sweden, as the biggest Western European country to do so, officially recognized the Palestinian state. Not surprisingly, this caused uproar in Israel, who immediately withdrew its ambassador from Stockholm, the Swedish capital.[136]

In the weeks leading up to Sweden's decision to recognize Palestine, Sweden's ambassador to Tel Aviv was called to Israel's Ministry of Foreign Affairs. Israel protested officially, telling the ambassador that Sweden's decision would harm rather than help the peace process between Israel and Palestine, and would create unrealistic expectations for the Palestinian people, who will come to believe that they can attain sovereignty without the need to negotiate with Israel.[137]

Sweden's Minister of Foreign Affairs Margot Wallström did not agree. The hope was, she said, that the move would add some dynamics to the stalled peace negotiations and grant young Palestinians new hope in a two-state solution. Recognizing Palestine as a legitimate state, she believed, would also contribute to decreasing the inequality between Israelis and Palestinians, which, in turn, would increase Palestine's responsibility to engage in appropriate political actions. But the question is whether upsetting one party to the conflict, in this case Israel, can really contribute to greater peace.[138]

To understand Sweden's decision to recognize Palestine, we must place it in historical context. The left-leaning parties in Sweden, most notably the Social Democratic Workers' Party which held power for the majority of the twentieth century, tend to side with Palestine. However, this was not always the case. For example, when Israel was a new state, the collective work on the kibbutz was viewed as admirable. But as the ties between Israel and the United States strengthened, the left-leaning parties in the world expressed their support for Palestine, while the right-leaning parties tended to support Israel. In the eyes of the left, Israel has transformed over time into a racist state.[139]

Sweden has long worked for a peaceful solution to the conflict between Israel and Palestine. For instance, in a speech in 1983, Sweden's former prime minister Olof Palme expressed solidarity with Israel, and stated his conviction that Israel is entitled to live in peace within secure and clearly defined borders. Simultaneously, he also praised Nahum Goldmann, the founder and longtime president of the World Jewish Congress, for his clear-sightedness several decades earlier, when he stated that the Jewish people's right to live in peace within a sovereign state cannot be fully realized until the Palestinian people, too, can live in peace and enjoy the right to a state they can call home.[140]

Sweden has traditionally had good diplomatic relations with Israel and engages regularly in economic affairs, cultural promotions, and research. Israel is Sweden's foremost business partner in the region, and several Swedish businesses are represented in Israel. Palestine, by contrast, is given large amounts of financial support from Sweden, which purpose is foremost to promote a democratic formation of a stable state that embraces freedom of religion, respect for human rights, and equal rights between women and men. Sweden also supports increased access to clean water and a better environment. However, Sweden has not had traditional diplomatic engagements with the West Bank and Gaza, since they are not officially recognized as a state. The belief is that the peace process cannot move forward, unless both Israel and Palestine act with basic human rights in mind and refrain from provocative actions. Sweden has participated since 1997 in a civilian observation of the West Bank with the intent to increase security for the inhabitants of Hebron. A high priority is to open Gaza's borders for humanitarian help.[141]

According to Wallström, then, Sweden is siding not with Palestine per se, but with the peace process. It is believed that the objectives can only be reached if Palestine can partake as a fully recognized partner at the negotiating table. The official recognition also means greater expectations of Palestine. Sweden holds that Palestine comprises a territory, a people, and a government. But the support for Palestine also comes with certain requirements, some of which include the promise that Palestine will fight corruption within, distance itself from violence, and support the rights of women. While this sounds good in theory, others question what Sweden's hidden agenda might be. What does Sweden have to win by recognizing Palestine? According to Wallström, taking a definite stand in the peace process will earn Sweden a better reputation worldwide. The decision lends support to the more moderate forces in a world that is increasingly leaning toward greater radicalization.[142] But why right now? Because now is the right time, said Wallström. Now is a critical time, now that violence has returned to Gaza.[143]

Although some say that the decision to recognize Palestine came too soon and others believe it came too late, Sweden views it as an important step that confirms Palestine's right to self-determination. The hope is that it will lead to a greater balance of political power, where Israelis and Palestinians can live peacefully side-by-side without one dominating the other, with mutually recognized borders from 1967 and Jerusalem as the capital for both states, and with exchanges of territories negotiated and approved by both states. The hope is also that recognizing Palestine as a legitimate state will have a stabilizing impact on the whole Middle Eastern region. Sweden wishes to give both young Israelis and Palestinians a future, where young men can find better alternatives than joining radical groups and engaging in terror. But a two-state solution also requires that Palestine has access to the necessary resources to build a viable state for its people.[144]

The European Union confirmed in 2009 its readiness to recognize Palestine when the time seemed right. According to Wallström, Sweden is ready to lead. In light of the difficult situation in the region and a long analysis of the Palestinian people's right to self-determination, the Swedish government can see no reason for further delay and hopes that the decision to recognize Palestine will motivate others to follow.[145]

That Israel and the United States would criticize Sweden's decision heavily was fully expected. Israel reacted by calling home Isaac Bachman, its ambassador to Sweden. Bachman said in an interview that the decision sends the wrong signal and will not enhance possibilities for peace. Instead, it will indicate to the Palestinians that terror attacks not only pay and will go unpunished, but will also be rewarded. Bachman did not view the inequality between Israel and Palestine as the root of the problem, or as having any effect on Palestine's willingness to negotiate for peace. In Bachman's view, the Israeli settlements in the occupied territories are not the reason for the conflict. Israel is not looking at the acquisition of additional territories, but is merely trying to survive against the continued violence in the region.

The hatred toward Israel by Palestine and other countries in the region started long before the settlements.[146]

Bachman further viewed the recognition of the Palestinian state as a one-sided act that excluded Israel and would benefit only the Palestinians. When asked how the decision would affect future relations between Sweden and Israel, Bachman said that he views Sweden's decision to recognize Palestine as separate from other relations, and hopes Sweden and Israel can continue to engage in trade, business, technology, and science. But the withdrawal of the ambassador is viewed as a clear protest by Israel against Sweden, and may deter other countries from following in Sweden's footprints.[147]

Zvi Mazel, the former Israeli ambassador to Sweden, expressed the view that Sweden has become one of the more radical countries in Europe working against Israel. Mazel, who is a controversial figure in Sweden, has spoken in the past of a "deep-rooted anti-Semitic sentiment that he says is inherent to Swedish culture," and has told a Swedish newspaper that "Sweden is among the most severely anti-Semitic places" with "daily agitations in the media to kill Jews." But according to Meir Horden, the Rabbi of Stockholm's Orthodox Jewish community in 2007, "[i]t's not true to say that the Swedes are anti-Semitic. Some of them are hostile to Israel because they support the weak side, which they perceive the Palestinians to be," and generally "Swedish support for the Palestinians comes from the same place that led the Swedes to help Holocaust survivors."[148]

Mazel's views may thus have roots in the fact that Sweden so strongly sympathizes with Third World countries, and many Swedes have difficulties viewing Israel as anything other than a neo-colonial entity. The sympathy for Third World countries grew from Sweden's former prime minister Olof Palme, who worked for the

Social Democratic Workers' Party for several decades, and who has become something of a folk hero after his assassination in 1986. Under Palme's leadership, Sweden distanced itself from mainstream European thinking and started to engage in the conflicts of the Third World. To those taking this view, Israel is the "bad guy," who wages war against the "good" poorer nations. The greater question might be why Sweden, who has no colonial burden to carry, in some people's view still has managed to feel a sort of "colonial guilt" that necessitates righting a past wrong by defending Third World countries against colonial powers, regardless of who might be in the right.[149]

Others argue that, from a human rights perspective, it is meaningless to acknowledge a Palestinian state unless the right of Israel to exist is also fully acknowledged. To recognize a Palestinian state before peace negotiations have taken effect and before Israel's legitimate security questions are answered, is equivalent to jeopardizing Israel's existence. It is also troublesome that the government that Hamas is thought to initiate would comprise at least one party with explicit anti-Semitic views, who distances themselves from human rights issues and whose main objective is the total annihilation of Israel as a state. The development of this decision could well be that Sweden's role as world defender of democracy and human rights will be severely harmed.[150]

Some Israelis take a different view, however, and believe that Sweden has been influenced by the large number of refugees from the Arab world. They also fear that Sweden's decision to officially recognize Palestine will give the Palestinians unrealistic expectations, since many Palestinians see as their objective to eradicate

Israel. Some Israelis also think that Sweden tends to get involved in the Israel-Palestine conflict without understanding that Palestine is a "terrorist state." Others take the opposite view and welcome Sweden's proactive stance. Some even acknowledge that the Israel occupation of Palestine territories has turned an otherwise humanitarian state into an obnoxious state. Thanks to Sweden's involvement, the issue is back in the public debate, which is a good thing, because many Israelis who live in the multi-cultural Tel Aviv are not even aware of the conflict that is going on around them.[152]

How did the Palestinians react when they heard the news? PGS (Palestina Grupperna i Sverige or the Palestinian Groups in Sweden) welcomed the new democratic socialist government's decision to follow the 134 countries in the United Nations who had already recognized Palestine as a state, and expressed hope that other countries in the European Union would follow. The recognition of Palestine came as great moral support for the Palestinian people and heightened their status on the world scene. It also demonstrated that Sweden is serious in its promise to work for the rights of the Palestinians. However, simply recognizing Palestine is not enough. In order to move forward and end the occupation, it is crucial that other countries, too, take a stand for Palestine and against Israel's current policies. PGS hopes that Sweden will end all military cooperation with Israel, and that Israel's crimes in light of international law will lead to sanctions.[152]

Palestine's Minister of Foreign Affairs Riad al-Malki, too, expressed his gratitude toward Sweden and the courage shown under intense pressure from other European countries. Sweden has long been viewed as one of the more Palestine friendly countries in Europe, and Israel has already long ago viewed Sweden as one of the more Israel-critical countries in Europe. The recognition of Palestine should therefore not come as a big surprise, and does not deviate markedly from decades of foreign policy choices Sweden has made in the past. When viewed in this light, however, it is questionable whether a small country such as Sweden can have any significant impact on the peace process.[153] There are also Palestinians who do not believe that Sweden's decision will have any positive effect for Palestine.[154]

Other countries within the region also expressed their views regarding the continuing struggle between Israel and Palestine. According to Radio Islam, there are three ways to view the Jewish state in Palestine. First is the view that the area has been promised the Jews by their god, and if Israel perishes, all Jews will also perish. Then is the view that most Western states hold, and which acknowledges Israel as an existing state since its recognition by the United Nations. According to this view, Israel is a political entity that exists in practicality and must therefore be accepted. Then is the view embraced mostly by Palestinians and Muslims, particularly in the Arab world, which holds that Israel has taken the land from the Palestinians through violence, and that Israel continues to enslave and oppress Palestine.[155]

Radio Islam further held that there are two valid reasons why Israel's enslavement of Palestine must end. First, it is a matter of human rights. No people should have the political right to oppress another by conquering their territory and enslaving them. Second, in order to solve the Israel-Palestine conflict, Palestine must be fully recognized. The only solution to this dangerous conflict is that the rest of the world take a definite stand and place political pressure on Israel, until the great majority of

Jews in Israel realize that Israel must allow Palestine its own territory, resources, and right to self-government. The problem is more than a local conflict between Israel and Palestine, which is why the rest of the world must care enough to take a definite stand. As long as Israel continues to terrorize Palestine, the Muslim hate for Israel and other countries that are friendly toward Israel will grow and threaten also the Western European countries.[156]

With the foregoing in mind, let us ask again why Sweden acted as it did at this particular point in time. It is speculated that Sweden might have received some signals that the official recognition of Palestine might start a dynamic action toward peace. But it is also speculated that it has more to do with domestic political reasoning, where Sweden's new government wishes to express a more left-leaning position.[157] And what is the attitude among the Swedish population in general? According to one source, although the Swedish government has the right to recognize Palestine, the decision lacks support among 56 percent of the Swedish people and has therefore not reached majority consensus. The Swedish government also lacks the support of its Nordic neighbors. The opposition notes that it is not possible for Sweden, who has not been to war in 200 years (since 1814) to fully understand the complicated issues surrounding human rights in practical terms.[158] Still others might argue that the reason why Sweden has not been involved in war in 200 years, is because the country has consistently acted with forethought and taken every step possible to avoid the military option before all diplomatic channels have been exhausted.

NOTES

[1]Olof Palme, "Därför Blev Jag Demokratisk Socialist (Why I Became a Democratic Socialist)," Mariefreds S-Förening, http://www.s-info.se/association/various.asp?id=554&page=3875&navi=8.

[2]Olof Palme, "Med Egna Ord: Samtal Med Serge Richard Och Nordal Åkerman (In My Own Words: Conversation with Serge Richard and Nordal Åkerman)," (Uppsala, Sweden: Bromberg, 1977).

[3]Palme, Svensk Dokumentär (Swedish Documentary) by Kristina Lindström and Maud Nycander, B-Reel Presenterar I Samproduktion Med Sveriges Television Film I Väst Med Stöd Av Nordisk Film & TV Fond (2012).

[4]Palme, "Med Egna Ord: Samtal Med Serge Richard Och Nordal Åkerman."

[5]Palme, Svensk Dokumentär.

[6]Palme, "Med Egna Ord: Samtal Med Serge Richard Och Nordal Åkerman."

[7]Olof Palme, *Att Vilja Gå Vidare (The Desire to Progress)* (Malmö, Sweden: Tidens Förlag, 1974), 244.

[8]Ibid. 154.

[9]Palme, "Med Egna Ord: Samtal Med Serge Richard Och Nordal Åkerman."

[10]Martin Tunström, "Tage Erlander Om Olof Palme" (Tage Erlander About Olof Palme)," YouTube, http://www.youtube.com/watch?v=IQ-ojUHBE9A&feature=related.

[11]Sofia Härén, "Reform För Rättvisa Och Miljö" (Reform for Justice and the Environment), *Miljömagasinet*, No. 33 (Aug. 20, 2010).

[12]Stellan Andersson, "SSU's Studieledare—Och Ideologiernas Betydelse" (SSU's Leader of Studies—and the Meaning of the Ideology), OlofPalme.org, http://www.olofpalme.org/personen/biografiska-notiser/1955/.

[13]Henrik Berggren, *Underbara Dagar Framför Oss: En Biografi Över Olof Palme (Wonderful Days Ahead of Us: A Biography of Olof Palme)* (Stockholm, Sweden: Norstedts, 2010), 157.

[14]Palme, Svensk Dokumentär.

[15]Berggren, 9-10.

[16]Palme, *Att Vilja Gå Vidare*, 28.

[17]Palme, "Med Egna Ord: Samtal Med Serge Richard Och Nordal Åkerman."

[18]Peter Antman, *Den Kämpande Demokraten: Olof Palmes Inrikespolitiska Idearv (The Struggling Democrat: Olof Palme's Domestic Policy View Inheritance)*, Internet Version (Mar. 2001), 18.

[19]Ibid., 16.

[20]Berggren, 311.

[21]Ibid., 333.

[22]Ibid., 260-261.

[23]Ibid., 299.

[24]Ibid., 341.

[25]Ibid., 423.

[26]Ibid., 422.

[27]Ibid., 642-643.

[28]Palme, *Att Vilja Gå Vidare*, 169.

[29]Berggren, 340.

[30]Antman, 21.

[31]Ibid., 30-31.

[32]Berggren, 340.

[33]Olof Palme, "Employment and Welfare," The 1984 Jerry Wurf Memorial Lecture, The Labor and Worklife Program, Harvard Law School, 16.

[34]Olof Palme, "Work, Justice, and Peace," *Olof Palme Speaking: Articles and Speeches* (The Olof Palme International Center and Premiss Förlag, 2006), 53.

[35]Berggren, 177.

[36]Olof Palme, "Social Justice and Individual Freedom," *Olof Palme Speaking: Articles and Speeches* (The Olof Palme International Center and Premiss Förlag, 2006), 50.

[37]Berggren, 351.

[38]Antman, 30.

[39]Berggren, 13-14.

[40]Ibid., 461.

[41]Gunnar Fredriksson, "Olof Palme," Swedish Institute (1986), 7-8.

[42]Ibid., 20.

[43]Berggren, 72.

[44]Palme, Svensk Dokumentär.

[45]Olof Palme, "The Welfare State," *Olof Palme Speaking: Articles and Speeches* (The Olof Palme International Center and Premiss Förlag, 2006), 60-61.

[46]Berggren, 335.

[47]Ibid., 340.

[48]Olof Palme, "The Right to Work," *Olof Palme Speaking: Articles and Speeches* (The Olof Palme International Center and Premiss Förlag, 2006), 74.

[49]Berggren, 284.

[50]Ibid., 203-204.

[51]Ibid., 648.

[52]Antman, 37.

[53]Ibid., 29.

[54]Berggren, 452.

[55]Ibid., 453.

[56]Ibid., 455-456.

[57]Ibid., 457.

[58] Antman, 40-42.

[59] Berggren, 206-207.

[60] Ibid., 207.

[61] Olof Palme, "The Struggle for Women's Liberation," *Olof Palme Speaking: Articles and Speeches* (The Olof Palme International Center and Premiss Förlag, 2006), 84.

[62] Antman, 39.

[63] Palme, "The Struggle for Women's Liberation," 83.

[64] Agneta Carleson, "Kvinnor I Palestina Vill Ha Jämställdhet (Women in Palestine Want Equality)," *Internationella Social Demokraten (The International Social Democrat)*, #2 (2010), 15.

[65] Berggren, 460.

[66] Ibid., 26.

[67] Ulla Richter, "Kvinnor Kan Förändra (Women Can Affect Change)," *Internationella Social Demokraten (The International Social Democrat)*, #2 (2010), 16.

[68] Olof Palme, "Child and Family Policy," *Olof Palme Speaking: Articles and Speeches* (The Olof Palme International Center and Premiss Förlag, 2006), 79.

[69] Ibid., 80.

[70] Jareen Imam, "Sweden Moves to Extend Paid Paternity Leave for Dads," *CNN* (May 30, 2015), http://www.cnn.com/2015/05/30/living/sweden-paid-paternity-leave/.

[71] Nick Visser, "Sweden is About to Give New Fathers a Third Month of Paid Paternity Leave," *Huffington Post* (May 28, 2015), http://www.huffingtonpost.com/2015/05/28/sweden-paternity-leave_n_7463530.html.

[72] Ibid., 462.

[73] Berggren, 496-497.

[74]Samantha Schroeder, "Swedish Toys R Us Franchise Goes Gender Neutral in Christmas Catalog," *Daily Caller* (Nov. 26, 2012), http://dailycaller.com/2012/11/26/swedish-toys-r-us-franchisee-goes-gender-neutral-in-christmas-catalog/.

[75]Ingvar Carlsson and Anne-Marie Lindgren, *What is Social Democracy: A Book About Ideas and Challenges*, Arbetarrörelsens Tankesmedja (Borås, Sweden: The Swedish Labour Movement Think Tank and The Olof Palme International Center, 2008), 23-24.

[76]Ananya Bhattacharya, "Sweden Flirts With Six Hour Work Day," *CNN Money* (Oct. 2, 2015), http://money.cnn.com/2015/10/02/news/economy/sweden-6-hour-work-day/index.html?iid=ob_homepage_money_pool&iid=obnetwork.

[77]Ibid.

[78]Berggren, 255.

[79]Carlsson and Lindgren, 49.

[80]Ibid., 68.

[81]Philip Rucker, "Mitt Romney Says Corporations Are People," *Washington Post* (Aug. 11, 2011), http://www.washingtonpost.com/politics/mitt-romney-says-corporations-are-people/2011/08/11/gIQABwZ38I_story.html.

[82]Antman, 47.

[83]Carlsson and Lindgren, 26.

[84]Antman, 65.

[85]Ibid.

[86]Ibid.

[87]Berggren, 33-36.

[88]Nancy Pelosi, "The Truth About Medicare," *Special to CNN* (Oct. 16, 2012), http://www.cnn.com/2012/10/15/opinion/pelosi-medicare/index.html?hpt=hp_c3.

[89]Berggren, 99.

[90]Ibid., 210.

[91]Ibid., 326-328.

[92]Ibid., 328-329.

[93]Antman, 30.

[94]Louis Jacobson, "Rick Santorum Calls Barack Obama a 'Snob' for Wanting 'Everybody in America to Go to Gollege,'" *Tampa Bay Times* (Feb. 27, 2012), http://www.politifact.com/truth-o-meter/statements/2012/feb/27/rick-santorum/rick-santorum-calls-barack-obama-snob-wanting-ever/.

[95]Carlsson and Lindgren, 25.

[96]Berggren, 526 & 529.

[97]Ibid., 542 & 544.

[98]Michael Grunwald, "The Party of No: New Details on the GOP Plot to Obstruct Obama," *Time* (Aug 23, 2012), http://swampland.time.com/2012/08/23/the-party-of-no-new-details-on-the-gop-plot-to-obstruct-obama/.

[99]Berggren., 242.

[100]Ibid., 258-259.

[101]Ibid., 242.

[102]Jennifer Heape, "Segregation Widespread for Swedish Immigrants," *The Local* (Dec. 18, 2008), http://www.thelocal.se/20081218/16452.

[103]Carlsson and Lindgren, 91.

[104]Michael Scheuer, "Oslo: Likely an Opening Act, Not a One-Off Event," Michael Scheuer's Non-Intervention.com (Jul 30, 2011), http://non-intervention.com/985/oslo-likely-an-opening-act-not-a-one-off-event/.

[105]Ralph Peters, *Never Quit the Fight* (Mechanicsburg, PA: Stackpole Books, 2006), 118.

[106]Thomas Peterffy, "Freedom to Succeed," YouTube (Oct. 12, 2012), https://www.youtube.com/watch?v=N2QtDExs6lM.

[107]Ibid.

[108]Berggren, 418.

[109]Palme, Svensk Dokumentär.

[110]Berggren, 158.

[111]Fredriksson, 9.

[112]Olof Palme, "Disarmament and Development," *Olof Palme Speaking: Articles and Speeches* (The Olof Palme International Center and Premiss Förlag, 2006), 93.

[113]Olof Palme, Interview with David Frost (1969), YouTube, http://www.youtube.com/watch?v=6KZXe2prBgU.

[114]Olof Palme, "The Middle East," *Olof Palme Speaking: Articles and Speeches* (The Olof Palme International Center and Premiss Förlag, 2006), 162-163.

[115]Palme, "Med Egna Ord: Samtal Med Serge Richard Och Nordal Åkerman."

[116]Berggren, 353 & 357.

[117]Palme, Svensk Dokumentär.

[118]Anna Lindh, "Än Kan Ett Krig Mot Irak Undvikas (Still Can a War Against Iraq Be Avoided)," *Aftonbladet* (Feb. 13, 2003).

[119]Thucydides, *The History of the Peloponnesian War*, Chapter XVII, translated by Richard Crawley, Project Gutenberg, http://www.gutenberg.org/files/7142/7142-h/7142-h.htm.

[120]Olof Palmes Minnesfond (Olof Palme's Memorial Fund), Olof Palme, 1977, http://www.palmefonden.se/index.php?&pid=27.

[121]Norraguldheden, "Olof Palme Mördad: Reaktioner (Olof Palme Murdered: Reactions)," YouTube, http://www.youtube.com/watch?v=SaNu2urUPU4.

[122]Abdul Karim Bangura, *Sweden vs. Apartheid: Putting Morality First* (Hants, England: Ashgate Publishing Limited, 2004), 95.

[123]Palme, "The Right to Work," 71-72.

[124]John Wagner, "Why Sanders May Not Enjoy His First Face-Off With Clinton as Much as He Might Expect," *Washington Post* (Oct. 13, 2015), https://www.washingtonpost.com/news/post-politics/wp/2015/10/13/sanders-has-been-looking-forward-to-time-on-stage-with-clinton-he-might-not-enjoy-it-as-much-as-he-expects/.

[125]Late Night with Seth Meyers, "Bernie Sanders Explains Why 'Socialist' is Not a Dirty Word," YouTube (Jun. 2, 2015), https://www.youtube.com/watch?v=BFAq-4Vv5c0.

[126]Chris Cillizza, "Bernie Sander's Liberty University Speech, Annotated," *Washington Post* (Sep. 14, 2015), http://www.washingtonpost.com/news/the-fix/wp/2015/09/14/bernie-sanders-liberty-university-speech-annotated/.

[127]Ibid.

[128]Richard North Patterson, "The Paradox of Bernie Sanders," *Huffington Post* (Oct. 5, 2015), http://www.huffingtonpost.com/richard-north-patterson/the-paradox-of-bernie-san_b_8240460.html.

[129]Frank Ninkovich, *The Wilsonian Century: U.S. Foreign Policy Since 1900* (Chicago, IL: The University of Chicago Press, 1999), 291.

[130]Palme, Svensk Dokumentär.

[131]Ibid.

[132]Ibid.

[133]Ibid.

[134]Victor Hugo, *Les Misérables* (New York, NY: Thomas Y. Crowell & CO, 1887), 240.

[135]YouTube, "Middle East Not IKEA Simple— Israeli Foreign Minister Avigdor Lieberman Snaps at Sweden Over Pales" (Oct. 31, 2014), https://www.youtube.com/watch?v=XBvnr9flTeE.

[136]Karl Ritter, "Sweden Recognizes Palestinian State," *The World Post* (Oct. 30, 2014), http://www.huffingtonpost.com/2014/10/30/sweden-palestinian-state_n_6074390.html.

[137]Robert Holender, "Hemliga Samtal Mellan Israel Och Sverige Om Palestina (Secret Conversations Between Israel and Sweden About Palestine)," *DN.SE* (Oct. 6, 2014), http://www.dn.se/nyheter/sverige/hemliga-samtal-mellan-israel-och-sverige-om-palestina/.

[138]Erik Melin, "Sveriges Regering Har Erkännt Staten Palestina (Sweden's Government has Recognized the Palestinian State)," *Aftonbladet*, http://www.aftonbladet.se/nyheter/article19776646.ab.

[139]Björn Björkqvist, "Ska Israel-Palestina-Konflikten Splittra Sverige? (Shall the Israel-Palestine Conflict Divide Sweden?)," *Realisten* (Jul. 15, 2014).

[140]Olof Palme, Arbetarrörelsens Arkiv och Bibliotek (Apr. 13, 1983), http://www.olofpalme.org/wp-content/dokument/830413_storkyrkan.pdf.

[141]Myndigheten För Samhällsskydd Och Beredskap, "Sverige Och Israel-Palestina (Sweden and Israel-Palestine)," säkerhetspolitik.se, http://www.sakerhetspolitik.se/Konflikter/Israel-Palestina/Sverige-och-Israel-Palestina/.

[142]Melin.

[143]Ibid.

[144]Margot Wallström, "Därför Erkänner Sverige I Dag Staten Palestina (Why Sweden Recognized the Palestinian State Today)," *DN.Debatt* (Oct. 30, 2014), http://www.dn.se/debatt/darfor-erkanner-sverige-i-dag-staten-palestina/.

[145]Ibid.

[146]YouTube, "Sverige Erkänner Palestina (Sweden Recognizes Palestine)." (Oct. 30, 2014), https://www.youtube.com/watch?v=NcqI3xMLHbQ.

[147]Ibid.

[148]Cnaan Liphshiz, "Anti-Semitism, in Sweden? Depends Who You're Asking," Haaretz (Nov. 9, 2007), http://www.haaretz.com/weekend/anglo-file/anti-semitism-in-sweden-depends-who-you-re-asking-1.232895.

[149]Cecilia Udden, "Godmorgon, Världen! (Good Morning, World!)" Sveriges Radio (Oct. 10, 2014), sverigesradio.se.

[150]Tuve Skånberg, et al. "Att Erkänna Palestina Skulle Skada Sverige (Recognizing Palestine Would Harm Sweden)," *SvD Opinion*, http://www.svd.se/opinion/brannpunkt/att-erkanna-palestina-skulle-skada-sverige_3984393.svd.

[151]Udden.

[152]Palestina Grupperna I Sverige (The Palestinian Groups in Sweden), http://www.palestinagrupperna.se/.

[153]YouTube, "Sverige Erkänner Palestina.

[154]Udden,

[155]Ahmed Rami, "Israels Makt I Sverige (Israel's Might in Sweden)," *Radio Islam*, radioislam.org.

[156]Ibid.

[157]YouTube, "Sverige Erkänner Palestina.

[158]Martin Blecher, "En Subjektiv Syn På Folkrätten (A Subjective View on Human Rights)," *nt.se* (Nov. 6, 2014).

BIBLIOGRAPHY

Andersson, Stellan. "SSU's Studieledare—Och Ideologiernas Betydelse" (SSU's Leader of Studies—and the Meaning of the Ideology). OlofPalme.org. http://www.olofpalme.org/personen/biografiska-notiser/1955/.

Antman, Peter. *Den Kämpande Demokraten: Olof Palmes Inrikespolitiska Idearv (The Struggling Democrat: Olof Palme's Domestic Policy View Inheritance).* Internet Version (Mar. 2001).

Bangura, Abdul Karim. *Sweden vs. Apartheid: Putting Morality First.* Hants, England: Ashgate Publishing Limited, 2004.

Berggren, Henrik. *Underbara Dagar Framför Oss: En Biografi Över Olof Palme (Wonderful Days Ahead of Us: A Biography of Olof Palme).* Stockholm, Sweden: Norstedts, 2010.

Bhattacharya, Ananya. "Sweden Flirts With Six Hour Work Day." *CNN Money* (Oct. 2, 2015). http://money.cnn.com/2015/10/02/news/economy/sweden-6-hour-work-day/index.html?iid=ob_homepage_money_pool&iid=obnetwork.

Björkqvist, Björn. "Ska Israel-Palestina-Konflikten Splittra Sverige? (Shall the Israel-Palestine Conflict Divide Sweden?)." *Realisten* (Jul. 15, 2014).

Blecher, Martin. "En Subjektiv Syn På Folkrätten (A Subjective View on Human Rights)." *nt.se* (Nov. 6, 2014).

Carleson, Agneta. "Kvinnor I Palestina Vill Ha Jämställdhet (Women in Palestine Want Equality)." *Internationella Social Demokraten (The International Social Democrat)*, #2 (2010).

Carlsson, Ingvar and Lindgren, Anne-Marie. *What is Social Democracy: A Book About Ideas and Challenges.* Arbetarrörelsens Tankesmedja. Borås, Sweden: The Swedish Labour Movement Think Tank and The Olof Palme International Center, 2008.

Cillizza, Chris. "Bernie Sander's Liberty University Speech, Annotated." *Washington Post* (Sep. 14, 2015). http://www.washingtonpost.com/news/the-fix/wp/2015/09/14/bernie-sanders-liberty-university-speech-annotated/.

Fredriksson, Gunnar. "Olof Palme." Swedish Institute (1986).

Grunwald, Michael. "The Party of No: New Details on the GOP Plot to Obstruct Obama." *Time* (Aug 23, 2012). http://swampland.time.com/2012/08/23/the-party-of-no-new-details-on-the-gop-plot-to-obstruct-obama/.

Härén, Sofia. "Reform För Rättvisa Och Miljö" (Reform for Justice and the Environment). *Miljömagasinet*, No. 33 (Aug. 20, 2010).

Heape, Jennifer."Segregation Widespread for Swedish Immigrants." *The Local* (Dec. 18, 2008). http://www.thelocal.se/20081218/16452.

Holender, Robert. "Hemliga Samtal Mellan Israel Och Sverige Om Palestina (Secret Conversations Between Israel and Sweden About Palestine)." *DN.SE* (Oct. 6, 2014). http://www.dn.se/nyheter/sverige/hemliga-samtal-mellan-israel-och-sverige-om-palestina/.

Hugo, Victor. *Les Misérables*. New York, NY: Thomas Y. Crowell & CO, 1887.

Imam, Jareen. "Sweden Moves to Extend Paid Paternity Leave for Dads." *CNN* (May 30, 2015). http://www.cnn.com/2015/05/30/living/sweden-paid-paternity-leave/.

Jacobson, Louis. "Rick Santorum Calls Barack Obama a 'Snob' For Wanting 'Everybody in America to Go to Gollege.'" *Tampa Bay Times* (Feb. 27, 2012). http://www.politifact.com/truth-o-meter/statements/2012/feb/27/rick-santorum/rick-santorum-calls-barack-obama-snob-wanting-ever/.

Late Night with Seth Meyers. "Bernie Sanders Explains Why 'Socialist' is Not a Dirty Word." YouTube (Jun. 2, 2015). https://www.youtube.com/watch?v=BFAq-4Vv5c0.

Lindh, Anna. "Än Kan Ett Krig Mot Irak Undvikas (Still Can a War Against Iraq Be Avoided)." *Aftonbladet* (Feb. 13, 2003).

Liphshiz, Cnaan. "Anti-Semitism, in Sweden? Depends Who You're Asking." Haaretz (Nov. 9, 2007). http://www.haaretz.com/weekend/anglo-file/anti-semitism-in-sweden-depends-who-you-re-asking-1.232895.

Melin, Erik. "Sveriges Regering Har Erkännt Staten Palestina (Sweden's Government has Recognized the Palestinian State)." *Aftonbladet*. http://www.aftonbladet.se/nyheter/article19776646.ab.

Myndigheten För Samhällsskydd Och Beredskap. "Sverige Och Israel-Palestina (Sweden and Israel-Palestine)." säkerhetspolitik.se. http://www.sakerhetspolitik.se/Konflikter/Israel-Palestina/Sverige-och-Israel-Palestina/.

Ninkovich, Frank. *The Wilsonian Century: U.S. Foreign Policy Since 1900*. Chicago, IL: The University of Chicago Press, 1999.

Norraguldheden. "Olof Palme Mördad: Reaktioner (Olof Palme Murdered: Reactions)." YouTube. http://www.youtube.com/watch?v=SaNu2urUPU4.

Olof Palmes Minnesfond (Olof Palme's Memorial Fund). Olof Palme, 1977. http://www.palmefonden.se/index.php?&pid=27.

Palestina Grupperna I Sverige (The Palestinian Groups in Sweden). http://www.palestinagrupperna.se/.

Palme, Olof. Arbetarrörelsens Arkiv och Bibliotek (Apr. 13, 1983). http://www.olofpalme.org/wp-content/dokument/830413_storkyrkan.pdf.

.........*Att Vilja Gå Vidare (The Desire to Progress).* Malmö, Sweden: Tidens Förlag, 1974.

........."Child and Family Policy." *Olof Palme Speaking: Articles and Speeches.* The Olof Palme International Center and Premiss Förlag, 2006.

........."Därför Blev Jag Demokratisk Socialist (Why I Became a Democratic Socialist)." Mariefreds S-Förening. http://www.s-info.se/association/various.asp?id=554&page=3875&navi=8.

........."Disarmament and Development." *Olof Palme Speaking: Articles and Speeches.* The Olof Palme International Center and Premiss Förlag, 2006.

........."Employment and Welfare." The 1984 Jerry Wurf Memorial Lecture. The Labor and Worklife Program. Harvard Law School.

.........Interview with David Frost (1969). YouTube. http://www.youtube.com/watch?v=6KZXe2prBgU.

........."Med Egna Ord: Samtal Med Serge Richard Och Nordal Åkerman (In My Own Words: Conversation with Serge Richard and Nordal Åkerman)." Uppsala, Sweden: Bromberg, 1977.

........."Social Justice and Individual Freedom." *Olof Palme Speaking: Articles and Speeches.* The Olof Palme International Center and Premiss Förlag, 2006.

........."The Middle East." *Olof Palme Speaking: Articles and Speeches.* The Olof Palme International Center and Premiss Förlag, 2006.

........."The Right to Work." *Olof Palme Speaking: Articles and Speeches.* The Olof Palme International Center and Premiss Förlag, 2006.

........."The Struggle for Women's Liberation." *Olof Palme Speaking: Articles and Speeches.* The Olof Palme International Center and Premiss Förlag, 2006.

........."The Welfare State." *Olof Palme Speaking: Articles and Speeches.* The Olof Palme International Center and Premiss Förlag, 2006.

........."Work, Justice, and Peace." *Olof Palme Speaking: Articles and Speeches.* The Olof Palme International Center and Premiss Förlag, 2006.

Palme. Svensk Dokumentär (Swedish Documentary) by Kristina Lindström and Maud Nycander. B-Reel Presenterar I Samproduktion Med Sveriges Television Film I Väst Med Stöd Av Nordisk Film & TV Fond (2012).

Patterson, Richard North. "The Paradox of Bernie Sanders." *Huffington Post* (Oct. 5, 2015). http://www.huffingtonpost.com/richard-north-patterson/the-paradox-of-bernie-san_b_8240460.html.

Pelosi, Nancy. "The Truth About Medicare." *Special to CNN* (Oct. 16, 2012). http://www.cnn.com/2012/10/15/opinion/pelosi-medicare/index.html?hpt=hp_c3.

Peterffy, Thomas. "Freedom to Succeed." YouTube (Oct. 12, 2012). https://www.youtube.com/watch?v=N2QtDExs6lM.

Peters, Ralph. *Never Quit the Fight*. Mechanicsburg, PA: Stackpole Books, 2006.

Rami, Ahmed. "Israels Makt I Sverige (Israel's Might in Sweden)." *Radio Islam*. radioislam.org.

Richter, Ulla. "Kvinnor Kan Förändra (Women Can Affect Change)." *Internationella Social Demokraten (The International Social Democrat)*, #2 (2010).

Ritter, Karl. "Sweden Recognizes Palestinian State." *The World Post* (Oct. 30, 2014). http://www.huffingtonpost.com/2014/10/30/sweden-palestinian-state_n_6074390.html.

Rucker, Philip. "Mitt Romney Says Corporations Are People." *Washington Post* (Aug. 11, 2011). http://www.washingtonpost.com/politics/mitt-romney-says-corporations-are-people/2011/08/11/gIQABwZ38I_story.html.

Scheuer, Michael. "Oslo: Likely an Opening Act, Not a One-Off Event." Michael Scheuer's Non-Intervention.com (Jul. 30, 2011). http://non-intervention.com/985/oslo-likely-an-opening-act-not-a-one-off-event/.

Schroeder, Samantha. "Swedish Toys R Us Franchise Goes Gender Neutral in Christmas Catalog." *Daily Caller* (Nov. 26, 2012). http://dailycaller.com/2012/11/26/swedish-toys-r-us-franchisee-goes-gender-neutral-in-christmas-catalog/.

Skånberg, Tuve, et al. "Att Erkänna Palestina Skulle Skada Sverige (Recognizing Palestine Would Harm Sweden)." *SvD* *Opinion*. http://www.svd.se/opinion/brannpunkt/att-erkanna-palestina-skulle-skada-sverige_3984393.svd.

Thucydides. *The History of the Peloponnesian War*, Chapter XVII. Translated by Richard Crawley. Project Gutenberg. http://www.gutenberg.org/files/7142/7142-h/7142-h.htm.

Tunström, Martin. "Tage Erlander Om Olof Palme" (Tage Erlander About Olof Palme)." YouTube. http://www.youtube.com/watch?v=IQ-ojUHBE9A&feature=related.

Udden, Cecilia. "Godmorgon, Världen! (Good Morning, World!)" Sveriges Radio (Oct. 10, 2014). sverigesradio.se.

Visser, Nick. "Sweden is About to Give New Fathers a Third Month of Paid Paternity Leave." *Huffington Post* (May 28, 2015). http://www.huffingtonpost.com/2015/05/28/sweden-paternity-leave_n_7463530.html.

Wagner, John. "Why Sanders May Not Enjoy His First Face-Off With Clinton as Much as He Might Expect." *Washington Post* (Oct. 13, 2015). https://www.washingtonpost.com/news/post-politics/wp/2015/10/13/sanders-has-been-looking-forward-to-time-on-stage-with-clinton-he-might-not-enjoy-it-as-much-as-he-expects/.

Wallström, Margot. "Därför Erkänner Sverige I Dag Staten Palestina (Why Sweden Recognized the Palestinian State Today)." *DN.Debatt* (Oct. 30, 2014). http://www.dn.se/debatt/darfor-erkanner-sverige-i-dag-staten-palestina/.

YouTube. "Middle East Not IKEA Simple—Israeli Foreign Minister Avigdor Lieberman Snaps at Sweden Over Pales" (Oct. 31, 2014). https://www.youtube.com/watch?v=XBvnr9flTeE.

........."Sverige Erkänner Palestina (Sweden Recognizes Palestine)." (Oct. 30, 2014). https://www.youtube.com/watch?v=NcqI3xMLHbQ.

About the author:

Martina Sprague has a Master of Arts Degree in Military History from Norwich University in Vermont. As an independent scholar, she has written numerous books about military and political/social history. She also writes instructional and analytical books on combat sports. For more information, please visit her Web site: www.modernfighter.com.

Other books of interest by Martina Sprague:

For God, Gold, and Glory: A History of Military Service and Man's Search for Power, Wealth, and Adventure

Leadership, It Ain't Rocket Science: A Critical Analysis of Moving with the Cheese and Other Motivational Leadership Bullshit

Sweden: An Illustrated History

Norse Warfare: Unconventional Battle Strategies of the Ancient Vikings

Swedish Volunteers in the Russo-Finnish Winter War, 1939-1940